HOW TO GET ALONG WITH DIFFICULT PEOPLE

FLORENCE LITTAUER

HARVEST HOUSE PUBLISHERS
Eugene, Oregon 97402

Cover by Left Coast Design, Portland, Oregon

HOW TO GET ALONG WITH DIFFICULT PEOPLE

Copyright © 1999 by Harvest House Publishers
Eugene, Oregon 97402

Library of Congress Cataloging-in-Publication Data
    Littauer, Florence, 1928–
        How to get along with difficult people / Florence Littauer. — Updated and expanded.
        p. cm.
    ISBN 1-56507-932-9
    1. Interpersonal relations—Religious aspects—Christianity.   2. Personality—Religious aspects—Christianity.   I. Title.
    BV4597.52.L58   1999
    248.4—dc21   98-43195
                                                         CIP

Printed in the United States of America.

05 /BP/ 10 9

A Personal Challenge

Is your life full of difficult people? "Then be happy, for when the way is rough, your patience has a chance to grow. So let it grow, and don't try to squirm out of your problems. For when your patience is finally in full bloom, then you will be ready for anything, strong in character, full and complete."[1]

The dictionary says *difficult* means: "Hard to understand or reach, painful, laborious, troublesome, puzzling, exacting, and stubborn."

Do you know any people who are difficult?

Is there one who's hard to understand or impossible to reach?

Is there a relationship that's painful?

Do you have a friend who's laborious, making a big deal out of nothing?

How about troublesome neighbors or puzzling relatives?

Do you have an exacting boss or stubborn children?

All of us know difficult people—now what are we going to do with them?

Contents

Marvin Music and Gertrude Grudge
Bob Bossy and Harriet Hurry
Larry Lazy
Sally Spiritual
Debbie Depressed
Joyce Judging and Gilda Guilt
Martha Martyr
Joe Jock
Winnie Witness

Compliments
Concern
Congratulations
Compromise
Choice
Challenge
Confidence

Introduction

Several years ago my husband Fred sent away for a present for me: a dozen pair of pantyhose at a discount price. They were labeled "slightly irregular" with flaws "barely perceptible to the human eye." The first 11 pairs seemed to have no problems at all, but then came the day when I took out that twelfth pair. I sat down to pull them on and found that there was only one leg! One little rear and one little leg! Isn't that more than "slightly irregular"? Isn't that flaw more than "barely perceptible to the human eye"? My daughter Lauren said immediately, "Send them back and get a new pair!" But I didn't return them because I knew they would make a great visual aid in speaking—and they have been.

When I'm talking about getting along with other people, I tell the story of the pantyhose and end by holding them up. Everyone laughs because they have never seen a one-legged pantyhose before. I then ask, "Isn't this more than slightly irregular?" As they nod I say, "Some of you may know people like this pantyhose who are more than slightly irregular." The audience groans. "Some of you may have married one of these!" They shriek.

My "slightly irregular" pantyhose make a clear point: All of us know people who are more than "slightly irregular." There are people who are impossible to get along with. Some are emotionally blind—they can't see our talents, skills, or successes. Some never give us compliments or credits. Some don't really hear what we're saying. Some cannot say "I'm sorry" or "It was my fault" or "Your were right." These are *difficult people* who don't see things our way.

Over the years women have given me new, slightly irregular pantyhose until I have quite a collection of hose that are worth absolutely nothing except as a humorous example. At the top of my one-legged hose is a sticker saying that these have been examined by Inspector 42 and found to be only slightly irregular. Don't you wonder what Inspector 42 looks like herself as she saw these to be only slightly irregular? How easy it is to judge other people from our own point of view and find those who don't agree with us have flaws more than barely perceptible to the human eye. In this book we will look at these difficult people and find out:

- Who they are.

- How they got that way.

- What their needs are.

- How we can deal with them.

Won't it be fun to observe the personalities of others and learn *How to Get Along with Difficult People!*

Chapter 1

Who Are the Difficult People?

Everyone knows some difficult people—they're everywhere. But who are they? Instead of talking about these people in generalities, let's create some characters we can see. Let's dress our principles in personality. Shakespeare said:

> All the world's a stage, and all the men and women merely players. They have their exits and their entrances; and one man in his time plays many parts.[2]

It is our pleasure once again to invite you to turn on your TV with that oversized screen in the sky and tune into the award-winning Christian daytime serial *Parade of Pious Personalities.* We get the picture into focus as we hear the Crystal Covenant Choir singing the theme song:

> Come, come, come, come,
> Come to the church in the valley,
> Come to the church in the vale.
> There's no church that's so dear to my childhood
> As the little brown church in the vale.

The voice of Tammy Talk, the telehost, trills "Thank you, thank you, thank you for tuning in today! Many of you listeners have been with us since we worshipped in the original Little Brown Church in the Vale before we built, with your generous contributions, the Big Brown Church on the Move. You may remember when Past-Pastor Paul Perfect was called to the pulpit and pondered over the pitiful plight of the church plant. You may be one of the thousands who responded to his plea for plentiful provision for God's people. You may be among those who received the snakeskin-covered Bible with your own initials in rhinestones at absolutely no charge when you sent in $10,000 to the building fund. Or you might be one who bought a brick at 500 dollars apiece, or a thousand dollars if you wanted your name etched on the brick before it was plastered in place personally by the parishioner who paid for it. So many of you listeners have been faithful to your pledges, so keep those cards and letters coming. Our new financial opportunity for this month will allow you to put a deposit on your own timeshare room, with a view of Mount Rushmore, in the Helen Brown Rice Retirement Residence, named for the daughter of our founder, Little Brown. The first hundred people rushing in their riches will receive a string of priceless pearl prayer beads as a generous gift reminding them to pray for the rest of the payments. Be among the first to secure your spot in the sanctity of this senior citizen city of tomorrow." Tammy smiles and flutters her eyelashes as the camera pulls back and replaces her with a scene of soft clouds with shining pearls on each one and a toll-free telephone number blinking at the bottom of the screen.

And now for our plot: Remember, in review, how Past-Pastor Paul Perfect produced a powerful church full of precious people, and then, according to the Peter Principle, he was taken from his place of prominence and elevated to the presidency of the Graduate School of Pastoral Profundity. The pulpit committee, tired of Pastor Perfect's sermons on Greek derivatives, searched for a new pastor with personality, and chose Sam Sermon from On-the-Mount Ministries.

The Big Brown Church prides itself on its people: blameless, harmless, and sinless. The bylaws state that no imperfect members will be admitted, although somewhere along the line a few difficult people drifted in.

Sally Spiritual

While Paul Perfect was pastor, the parish was kept pure, but when Sam Sermon was selected, he didn't seem to care who came to church as long as they contributed. As Sister Sally Spiritual says, "We gave him an inch and he took a mile." Sally always has words of wisdom to share with anyone who'll listen. She's always the first one in on Sunday morning to make sure the sanctuary is set up properly. She's tried to delegate the responsibility, but no one does it right. She personally created the chartreuse altar cloth and embroidered Adam and Eve in gold holding a basket of red apples. Sally is always glad to explain to visitors the symbolism expressed by this creative stitchery: that if we reach for one sin, we may soon have a basketful.

Sally is the only one allowed to conduct tours of the church, as the original was built by her grandfather Silas Spiritual in 1902, and her mother, Sadie Spiritual, played the organ from the day it was installed until her untimely death the day after she won the Senior Citizen Scripture Contest at the District Convention.

To begin the *Parade of Pious Personalities* on this Sunday morning, we see Sally arriving early to open up the church. As she always says, "It's the early bird that catches the biggest worms." You will notice that Sally, as usual, is wearing biblical black from head to toe. Her classic Christian hat is adorned by a lowly lily of the field and is modestly veiled. As superintendent of the Sunday School, Sally always carries coordinating black leather Bibles and a concordance for easy reference. Sally's only jewelry is a large cross, immediately identifying her as a believing Christian to the heathen world that spurns.

Sally has been a Christian for as long as she can remember. Right from her childhood, Sally was spiritual. She never desired any worldly possessions and never was tempted by the lusts of the flesh. Sally never smoked or drank; she never swore or gossiped; she never played cards or sewed on Sunday. Frankly, Sally is often shocked by the sins of others, and she prays for many fallen friends, plus a few heathen in China.

Sally knows all the spiritual greats of the century, and she loves to tell how her mother once dated Billy Graham's cousin and how her grandfather once bought shoes from D.L. Moody. It brings tears to her eyes to realize she was in the same elevator with Emilie Barnes at the Sunday School convention but was too stunned to get her autograph.

Sally spends much of her time in church, for, as she always says, "When the cat's away, the mice will play." On Monday nights she attends the pastor's Bible study on "The Deeper Pleasures of Personal Piety." On Tuesday nights she goes to the Missionary Society, where she is president of the Prudish Priscilla Circle. On Wednesday nights she rushes over to the prayer meeting, where the current topic is "Is Heaven for the Hindu?" On Thursdays she has to go early to pass out the books at choir rehearsal, where director Marvin Music is putting spiritual words to *Phantom of the Opera* to create a clever cantata for Christmas. On Fridays Sally has to bring a casserole to the Pioneer Girls' Potluck Supper and Sing-along, and on Saturday nights she has to chaperone the Teen Taco Treat and Hayride.

Today is Sunday, her busiest day of the whole week. She rises early to bake cookies for the coffee break. Since Sally is the only one with a complete set of keys to every door and cupboard, she must be "Johnny-on-the-spot." See her clanking ring of keys, which she has already used to open up the high-arched front door, hand-carved by her Uncle Creative. She now must check the chairs for junior church and then unlock the closet for the choir robes.

Some people have suggested that Sally should not have so much responsibility, but she always says, "If you can't count on the granddaughter of the man who built the church, whom can you ever count on?"

Sally's life is dedicated to the church, and she can recite the whole book of Philemon, but some people find her difficult.

Marvin Music

Sally jumps as she hears her name called in the empty church. It is Marvin Music, who needs the keys to the organ and choir cabinet. As Sally hands him the keys, she reminds Marvin, "It was my mother who played this organ brilliantly for 47 years until her untimely death...."

"Yes, I've heard." Marvin has no time for trivia, and he finds Sally especially offensive.

He always seems preoccupied, Sally muses, but he sure does dress well. Indeed, Marvin is a perfectionist. His pin-striped three-piece suit is a classic, his white shirt is so starched it could stand without him, and his tie is adorned with notes forming the first line of "The Old Rugged Cross." Marvin always carries the sheet music for the choir because "you can't trust anyone else."

Marvin checks his pockets. He has his three black pens: fine tip, medium tip, and felt tip. He has his collapsible baton and pointer, and his penlight in case he ever has to conduct in the dark. Marvin is prepared for any possible disaster and always expects the worst. He has his music planned out from now through Christmas and feels if anything's worth doing, it's worth doing right.

Here comes Pastor Sam Sermon. Marvin can't stand Sam because he's so sloppy and keeps changing his mind about the order of the service and expects Marvin to be flexible. Artistic people need to think and plan ahead. They shouldn't be expected to change at the last minute what they've practiced all week. Marvin is always right, but some people find him difficult. Marvin retreats to the choir loft so he won't have to talk to Sam.

Sam Sermon

Sam Sermon bounces up to the platform, singing off-key, totally oblivious to Marvin cringing in the choir loft. Sam always comes on too strong for Marvin, and he never seems to have his act together. He ran out of gas this morning and had to walk from the corner. As he hunts for his sermon notes in his over-stuffed briefcase, he throws everything out on the platform until he finds the McDonald's napkin where he had jotted down his thoughts while out for an Egg McMuffin with his 2-year-old son.

Sam doesn't believe in detailed notes—they only confuse you—and half the fun of preaching is making it up while you're on your feet. You never go stale that way.

Sam's hair is sticking out like a briarbush from his walk in the wind, and his green tie is crooked, but who will be able to take their eyes off his red, black and white plaid sportcoat long enough to notice? Sam was brought up in a church where the pastor wore a black robe, and he vowed if *he* ever had a congregation of his own he'd wear bright clothes to cheer up the parishioners.

Just looking at Sam depresses Marvin, who clears his throat and sings his scales. Sam jumps, knocking his glass of water onto his napkin of notes. "Now you've ruined my sermon," he cries out.

"It won't be the first time your sermon's been ruined," Marvin muses.

Marvin wonders if Sam will ever grow up. He was voted most likely to succeed in college, but he's never lived up to his potential. Sam's never had a knack for numbers, and he feels that balancing a checkbook is a waste of time. "It's either there or it isn't," he chuckles. Usually it isn't. Sam is frequently short of money, and he goes to the men's room when it's time for the waitress to bring the check. "God loves a cheerful giver," he reminds his friends. Sam still doesn't understand why the finance chairman quit when he found Sam had taken money from the World Hunger Fund to entertain his children at the San Diego Zoo. Marvin thinks to himself, "Sam's sermons are funny, but they seldom have a clear point, and he often runs overtime. When he goes too long, he just tells me to cut the music." Sam loves people and hugs everyone on his way to the front pew, but he can never remember their names. Sam shrugs, "What difference does it make? I just call them all 'honey' and they love me."

And most of them do, but some people such as Marvin find Sam difficult.

Joyce Judging

Most vocal in criticizing the pastor and parishioners is Joyce Judging, who comes from a long line of people with discerning spirits. As far as Joyce is concerned, the Christian life is a long list of don'ts for other people, and she feels that God has appointed her as the watchdog of the community. Joyce has a great memory for biblical instruction, and she feels led to tell other people where they are wrong and how they could improve to be like her. She loves to teach on the gifts of the Spirit and to show how she was personally anointed by the Lord Himself with the gifts of correction and direction.

She loves to tell how the Lord Himself led her down a dim alley to a pawn shop in Tel Aviv, where she found the original marble tablet of Moses saying "Thou shalt not." During the week she keeps it on her mantel at home as a warning to her children, lest they stray from the straight and narrow, but on Sundays she carries it with her as a sign of obedience.

This morning (as usual) Joyce is wearing pristine white to emphasize her purity. Joyce often shares at prayer meeting that her husband is not really a Christian, and she has pointed out to the children, "Daddy is not one of us!" Joyce knows so much more about God's laws than her husband that she feels called to point out his faults. She tells him constantly what a miserable sinner he is. She won't ever let him relax in his own home, and she nags him daily about his personal habits that hinder his hope for heaven. All their marriage problems are his fault, and she knows she could someday be happy if only *he* would shape up.

Joyce plays the organ on Sunday morning because it gives her the best vantage point from which to view the audience. Those she can't see over her left shoulder she can pick up in the mirror. "It's amazing what people will do when they don't think anyone is looking," Joyce confides to Marvin. Joyce confides a lot to Marvin. In fact, she sits next to him as often as possible. Since her husband isn't well, Joyce believes it's always good to have a Plan B firmly in mind, just in case.

Joyce Judging is always open to learning new truths, and this very afternoon she, Marvin Music, and the entire choir will be attending the new symposium "Music in Your Mid-Life Crisis." Joyce has taken courses on the "Inner Life," the "Outer Life," and the "Upper Life."

She has been baptized, sanctified, catechized, confirmized, and mesmerized, but all that her religious training seems to have done is provide her with a larger yardstick by which to measure the sins of other people.

Joyce is sincere, studious, and sinless—on the surface—but there are some people who find her superiority difficult.

Bob Bossy

It's now 10:45, and Dr. Bob Bossy drives up to the front door in his Mercedes and parks at the foot of the steps, blocking the sidewalk. He feels the "No Parking" sign is to keep other people out of his spot. Everyone knows he's the busiest doctor in town and must have his car available in case of emergencies. You'll notice he has the church ledgers in his arms so he can give a report to Sam Sermon before the service. He has his beeper on his belt to buzz him if a baby should want to be born between "Brighten the Corner" and the benediction. No one knows he can activate the beeper by himself, so if church goes overtime or he's in a dull meeting, he taps the unit and off it goes. Why, there it goes now!

People are in awe of Dr. Bossy's busy lifestyle and the money bags he carries for the week's deposits, and Sam Sermon is impressed with his position and prestige. With just one call to the bank he was able to get a loan large enough to build a basketball court out of the ladies' parlor and mount a new steeple higher than the one on the Baptist Church across the street. Sam appointed Bob chairman of the Board of Elders, and his first move was to make a large chart—which he carries with him—delineating everyone's area of control. Some who had been on the board for years were shocked to find they had responsibilities. "It's about time this place was run as a business," Bob stated at the annual meeting. "Until we get the budget balanced we're going to cut out air conditioning and charge for communion."

Bob Bossy is busy balancing the budget and controlling Sam but has little time for his family or friends. In spite of his money, some people find Dr. Bossy difficult.

Debbie Depressed

As we watch, Dr. Bossy lays down his moneybags and reviews the ledgers with Sam, Joyce Judging mulls over her music at the organ, Marvin Music agonizes over his anthems, Sally Spiritual rearranges her Bibles, and Sam Sermon desperately tries to reconstruct his sermon notes. The noise we hear is Debbie Depressed driving up in her old Dodge with the dents. Oh my, she's really depressed this morning as she didn't bother to get dressed. The last time she came to church in her bathrobe with those fuzzy old slippers, Marvin Music was furious. But she pointed out that the choir robe covers her up so what difference does it make how she looks? She leaves her pink rollers in until it's time to march in so the curl will last through lunch. She has a bag of cookies with her in case her blood sugar drops, and you'll notice that even her stuffed dog looks depressed. Her own personal black cloud hovers over her as she walks up the aisle to the choir loft. She's really too tired to sing, but she's afraid if she stays home people will talk about her—and they probably would. Debbie finds it difficult to make decisions, and when friends ask her out, she has to pray about it for weeks. Her favorite verse is Job 10:1 TLB: "I am weary of living." Debbie gets depressed over every little thing. She's weighed down with her weight, but she's too weary to exercise and hopes to drown her pounds in milk shakes. Nothing ever goes right for Debbie. She's the black sheep of the family. Her father wanted a boy, and her mother has never liked her.

The thought of housework overwhelms her. She gets discouraged over baskets of wrinkled laundry, but she can't bring herself to iron. One day she forced herself to clean the whole house, but no one noticed, so she quit. Much of the time Debbie pulls down the shades and won't answer the phone. She weeps in loneliness, but she really doesn't like people. She is a full-time counsel-seeker and details her depression to anyone who'll listen. Just last week when Evangelist Billy Braggart had a revival, Debbie rededicated her life each night, but she never seemed to improve.

Debbie is frequently ill, but the doctors can't find anything wrong. Her husband says it's all in her head, and she sighs, "No one really knows what I go through." Debbie has pills to pep her up and pills to calm her down. She takes them all to balance out her day. Each afternoon she watches the soaps and hopes someday to be healed by *General Hospital.* She always needs the pastor's counsel, and just yesterday she said to him, "I might as well just end it all, but I'm afraid no one would come to the funeral."

Sam feels sorry for Debbie, but some people find her difficult.

Harriet Hurry

As Debbie settles down to pour out her problems to Sam, we see Harriet Hurry running down the aisle in her Christian Dior jogging suit and matching Nike shoes. Since Harriet is always in a hurry, she wears a large clock so she can keep track of the time while on the run and several watches set to the times of the major capitals of the world. Harriet is an extremely competent lady, and no one knows how she finds the time to be the coordinator of Manna on Wheels, director of Hemming for Heathens, a member of the board of the Current Crucial Crises Council, and president of the Spiritual Jogging Society. She often rushes into a meeting late, gives a dramatic report, and leaves early to make it to the next meeting. Harriet's theme song is "I'm late, I'm late, for a very important date."

Harriet is out to save the world, and her husband calls her "The Lone Arranger." Harriet spends every Monday morning coordinating her calendars, and she has to check each day's schedule carefully. If you were to ask her out for lunch, she would not have a free day until the year 2050.

Harriet thrives on activity. If she can't find some, she'll create some. She is constantly moving furniture, redecorating the living room, or pouring a cement patio on the back yard. Harriet feels her friends and family are all lazy, and she is always trying to whip them into shape. She keeps a timer with her so she can check her children at their chores and constantly press them into improving their efficiency.

Harriet is too busy to be a real friend or to think a deep thought. Someday she'll have time for Bible study. Someday she'll have time for her children. Someday she'll have time for cooking.

Until then, the family will have to get along on Big Macs and Lean Cuisine.

Harriet may look a little casual for Sunday, but she only runs the nursery, and what do those babies care about her outfit?

Harriet can get more done in a shorter time than anyone in church, but some people find her difficult.

Martha Martyr

Here comes Martha Martyr, bringing out the trays of communion cups. It's her job to keep them clean, and she takes her duties very seriously. On Sundays Martha wears a conservative high-necked dress, lest she cause the church men to lust in their hearts. Martha never wears makeup, lest she appear worldly, and never a smile, lest she seem frivolous. Martha considers the Christian life to be one of extreme self-sacrifice and service to others. She always carries coordinating mops, pails, cloths, and cleaners to church in order to polish the communion table and pulpit. While Martha is not concerned with the latest fashions, she is always scrupulously clean and prepared for the daily duties that drop upon her.

Martha is always willing to stop scrubbing long enough to tell you about the time she washed all the diapers for the pastor's new baby even though she had a migraine headache.

She is the only deaconess who will scrub the church basement floor, and she does the dishes at each church supper after all the others have gone home and abandoned her. You can be sure that when Martha has done the dishes you will be able to see your face reflected in each plate.

Martha entertains all the visiting missionaries who pass through town because no one else really wants them. She feeds them simple food so they won't get spoiled before going back to the mission field. She collects old clothes for the missionaries (who, frankly, dress better than Martha).

Martha is a fanatical housekeeper, and she is constantly picking lint off furniture and friends, and especially Sam Sermon, who never looks quite put together. She rushes to fluff up the pillows the minute a person gets up from her couch, and she straightens pictures in everybody's home. Martha cooks constantly, and she recently preserved 40 jars of her specialty, "Mustard Seed and Okra." Her children are all fat, and she makes them sit at the table until they have stuffed down every last bite. If one child dares to object, Martha gives a mournful tale about all the poor, starving children in China. Martha constantly hovers over her husband, hands him his fork, cuts up his meat, and tells him of all her friends who don't really care for their men. Martha bleaches her husband's underwear, mends all his socks, and even presses his permanent-press shirts. Martha tells everyone how hard she works and what a noble mother she really is. Frankly, Martha is weary in well-doing and sighs a lot, but underneath she is so eager for the credit that she would rather die dusting than train a child to work.

Martha does every job at church that no one else will do and then tells Sam Sermon about it so he will praise her from the pulpit. Martha has an endless need for affirmation, especially from people of prestige. Martha's life seems full of ups and downs. One moment she's weighed down with the cares of the world, and the next she's giving a dramatic presentation of some personal problem in her past. Martha hides nothing from her friends, who have heard endless stories of her deprived childhood. She has told them so often of her years of malnutrition that they feel guilty when they eat. She always has the church ladies in tears on testimony night when she tells of how her drunken father ran off with the town floozy, leaving her consumptive mother with the 11 children, just the day before the tornado took the house.

Martha is overworked, overwrought, and overdone, and she slumps down to rest quite often. The church doesn't know what it would do without Martha Martyr, but some people find her difficult.

Larry Lazy

It's almost time for church to start, and Larry Lazy isn't here yet to pass out the bulletins. Larry never likes to get involved in church activities, but he can always see how other people could have done it better. He did agree to come once a month and be an usher because it seemed about the easiest thing to do (and one should help out one's local church). Larry never gets enthused about any of the programs, and when he heard they were planning a workday for all men to put up the steeple, he threatened to leave the church if he was required to come.

Larry's a pleasant fellow—in fact here he is now, ambling up the front steps in his cords and a sweater. He's passing out the bulletins and smiling at all the ladies, who find his cool, laid-back look appealing.

His wife, however, shared at Women's Confession Circle last week that she couldn't get him off the couch since he got the remote control for the TV. Their grass is up to the windowsills, and the outside ivy is crawling in through the cracks in the windows. Larry says he's waiting until they come out with robot lawnmowers, and he feels the invading ivy is attractive and saves on watering houseplants. Last week a piece of the roof fell in over the baby's bed, but he told his wife to pretend it was a skylight. It drives his wife crazy that he makes light of serious problems, but the other women think he's adorable.

Everybody loves Larry Lazy, but some people who have to rely on him find him difficult.

Winnie Witness

Here comes Winnie Witness on her way to teach her second-grade Sunday school class. She's full of pep and energy and always wears a skirt of many colors and her red T-shirt, which reads "Expect a Miracle." Winnie looks perpetually for potential converts and smiles all the time so people will ask how they can be happy like her.

Notice that Winnie is carrying a complimentary straw basket filled with hundreds of different evangelistic tracts. She has the plan of salvation in 12 languages and is willing to witness to the uttermost parts of the world.

To accent her stunning outfit, Winnie is wearing a pair of plastic Good News Gloves. By having her gloves on, she is always ready to explain God's plan in living color to any little lost child who doesn't know Jesus. Each finger on the glove is a different color: Green is the lost child, yellow is God's love, black is for sin, red is Christ's death, and white says, "I receive Him."

You would never guess that Winnie is a new Christian. She's the chairman of the Church Evangelism Committee even though she just became a believer at last spring's retreat at Pinkney Pines. When she came down the hill bursting with her new faith, she drove right over to her mother-in-law's home and told her that she was a sinner not yet saved by grace, that she attended a shallow church, and that she'd better leave her liberal denomination immediately.

Winnie then informed her husband that she would no longer go to the church of his youth because she didn't even think the pastor was a Christian. She immediately shared her faith with her husband, using the newest witnessing booklet. When he wouldn't pray with her, she told him he was hopeless, and she would shake the dust off her feet and go.

Today, as every day, Winnie was up early and out of the house seeking the lost. Her beds are unmade, and the dishes are in the sink, but she is witnessing aggressively to everyone she meets. Winnie grabs people wherever she find them, backs them against the wall, and asks, with a persuasive smile, "Is there any reason you would not want to become a Christian my way, now?" She turns everything into a time of testimony, and when her friends see her coming, they flee in the opposite direction. Winnie is determined to bring her husband into the kingdom, so she tapes verses to his mirror, puts big Bibles under his pillow, and hides tracts in his lunch pail. She must get to her Sunday school class, so she bustles off, giving a big smile and a wave to those already in the pews.

Winnie got an A in assertion training, but some people find her difficult.

Joe Jock

Winnie turns to see one of her new converts coming to church for the first time. Joe Jock is 6 feet 6 inches tall. He's arrived at the Big Brown Church in his gym clothes. Winnie wants to show him off, so she walks him down the aisle while smiling at everyone. Joe is strikingly handsome, like a Greek god. Winnie tells him so, and he whispers that he's modeled for art classes, been the inspiration for the marble statue of Alexander the Great on the town green, and been on many TV shampoo and cologne commercials.

Wow!

Joe's whole interest in life is his body and sports. As a boy he used the crib as a trampoline and lifted rattles to develop his muscles. In grammar school he was captain of every team, and in high school he earned every letter and sweater available. He won an athletic scholarship to Anxious State, where he majored in physical education. Each morning he was up at 5:30 working out with weights before going to his classes in Prevention of Muscular Atrophy and Inclement Weather Activities. For Joe an exciting date is going to college track meets, hosting tailgate picnics at the Auburn-Ole Miss football game, or watching videos of old Mike Tyson fights.

Now he has marked off the grass in his front yard and has coached his children and the neighborhood kids to play soccer. He is charging the parents to watch.

Winnie remembers how she met Joe at the gym, where she'd gone to evangelize the ladies who had weight problems. He'd been leading the group and noticed her exercising in her Good News Gloves. When he asked her what her button meant that said "WWJD," she said it stood for "What Would Jesus Do?" He responded, and Winnie led him to the Lord. That day Winnie met him in the gym, Joe was ready for a new life. His wife had walked out on him—Joe Jock, a hero! She'd told him she was sick of life being a series of World Series. She was no longer willing to be awash with the Lakers, depressed with the Dodgers, or anguished over the Angels. She didn't care if McGwire ever hit another home run and that for her, the Embraceable Ewes were a pasture of sheep. She'd had it.

So here's Joe in church. He can't believe it himself. Every girl has been crazy about him, but his ex-wife finds him difficult.

Gloria Gossip

The choir is now gathering for its entrance, dressed in new red robes bought with money raised from the sale of bumper stickers that say: "Get in the Groove, Join the Church on the Move."

The trio performing this morning is the "G-Clef Girls" with Gloria Gossip, Gilda Guilt, and Gertrude Grudge. Here comes

Gloria now. Gloria considers herself the historian of the church, and she carries a steno pad with her to jot down any new fact or fable. In fact, many of the favorite fables of the church would never have been passed down if it hadn't been for Gloria Gossip. She loves to both listen and talk and always makes her tales so tantalizing that people ask for more. She has a pillow on her couch that reads, "If you have nothing good to say about anyone, sit next to me."

Gloria has never let the truth stand in the way of a good story, and she believes if you tell her a dull tale, it is only right that she improve it enough so the next person won't be as bored with it as she was hearing it from you.

Gloria always writes in pencil so she can erase the facts if she comes up with a better ending to a tragic story. She prints up the secret prayer requests to pass out to all those who have the gift of intercession.

Gloria has trained herself to hear a different conversation with each ear while moving another one out of her mouth. It took years of practice to develop her three-track talent, and she's proud of her ability. She coordinates the church activities and sends out the monthly newsletter full of creative and colorful capers of the church family. Gloria mingles fact with fiction and makes the whole thing fun.

People look forward to her prayer requests and love to read her latest letter, but those who have been hurt by her gossip find her difficult.

Gilda Guilt

Gilda Guilt has her own quiet ministry: manipulation by guilt. She always says, "If you can make people feel guilty, you'll have them under control." When she and her friends go shopping or to meetings, Gilda always drives because the one with the car can always call the shots and be in charge. She teaches guilt classes at guild meetings and shows people how to subtly seize the steering wheel of life.

Gilda's carries her new book, *Gilda's Guide to Guilt,* which lists pages of manipulative phrases such as these:

To make grandmothers visit more say:

> "The poor little children hardly remember what you look like. But it's all right since their other grandmother is here so often."

To slow down people in a hurry say:

> "I thought you'd at least have time to look at my new bathroom wallpaper."

To get someone else to have Christmas say:

> "I guess I'd better start my Christmas preparations early because I always seem to get stuck with making the dinner, and it ruins my whole day."

To keep people visiting longer say:

> "Leave now? Why, you just sat down."

To get people to come who've already said no say:

> "It's too bad you can't come; I was going to give you a present."

To adult children who won't come to visit say:

> "It's a shame you can't come. I guess I'll have to make out my new will by myself."

Gilda is proud of her book full of comments about local people. "Once you have a book published," Gilda says, "You become an authority and people have to listen to you."

This week Gilda has a church contest in Gloria's newsletter for the best new idea in instilling guilt. She plans to write the most quotable sayings on squares of cloth in liquid embroidery and sew them together into a Guilt Quilt to be auctioned off at the Mother-Daughter Banquet.

Gilda often quotes the book *How to Be a Jewish Mother* where it says you must instill guilt in your children so they'll support you in your old age.

The church applauds her creativity, but those who have been manipulated once too often find Gilda difficult.

Gertrude Grudge

The third member of the "G-Clef Girls" is Gertrude Grudge. Remember when Gertrude first came to church carrying that huge black book and we all thought it was an oversized large-print Bible? We could tell it was covered in Morocco leather, but it took Gloria Gossip only a few minutes to inch over and read the gold embossed letters RECORD OF WRONGS.

Gertrude carries this book for more than its looks, as it contains the names of every single person who has ever wronged her. Gertrude has a brilliant and retentive mind, and her motto is "Never forgive and never forget." To make sure her facts are accurate, she jots down each problem as it occurs, and she has a special section for those people whom even the Lord Himself wouldn't forgive. Gertrude started her book at the age of five as only a precocious child could do. Her first entry was recorded in big print and quotes Aunt Violet, whom she overheard saying, "Poor Gertrude is a homely girl. I do hope she grows out of it."

She remembers how her first-grade teacher would not let her write on the board in colored chalk, and how disappointed she was when she tried out for the role of the rose in the Flower Festival and Miss Dimlick cast her as the thistle. Gertrude remembers how in high school she tried out for cheerleading and the coach put her on the football team. Gertrude has recorded every time she heard her mother-in-law say, "I can't imagine what he ever saw in her in the first place." She has down the name of the nurse who brought in her first baby and said, "They're all ugly in the beginning."

Gertrude knows how many Saturdays her husband watched football when she wanted him to clean the garage, and she has pages of dates when he came home late for dinner. She has many notes on how ungrateful her children are, even after she's stuffed their lunch boxes with Twinkies and softened their shirts with Downy.

She has recorded the past president of the Women's Club, who forgot to give Gertrude credit for decorating the entire stage for the opening tea, and also the one who did not put her name on the bronze plaque after she had given all the money for the new tea chairs. Gertrude remembers the name of the art chairman, who refused to exhibit the Grudge family paintings in the west alcove of the Clubhouse, and the Literary Section leader, who refused to print Gertrude's poem "Ode to an Elk" in the club bulletin.

Before coming to the Big Brown Church on the Move, Gertrude was the communion cloth chairman of St. Agony's parish. The pastor never did learn her name, and he called her Gertrude Frudge. The choir director would not let her sing a solo on Easter Sunday, the Christian education pastor left her name off the program as the prompter for the Christmas pageant, and the youth leader forbade her from coming to the teen campfire, even after she had donated the marshmallows. So poor Gertrude had no choice but to change churches. Gertrude keeps her *Record of Wrongs* with her at all times lest she forget or be tempted to forgive. Life has been difficult and thankless for Gertrude, but she just grins and records, knowing that at the great day of judgment she will jump up first with the biggest list.

The church admires her memory, but those whose names are in the book consider Gertrude to be difficult.

How great it is that Gloria, Gilda and Gertrude found each other and now provide harmony for all the difficult people in this perfect church.

Chapter 2

What Hope Is There for Understanding Others?

What hope is there for the Big Brown Church on the Move? They have a new sanctuary, a magnificent organ, the Crystal Covenant Choir, the G-clef girls, a basketball court, and the tallest steeple in town, but the church is filled with difficult people.

Sam Sermon means well and has charisma in the pulpit, but he has no idea how to pull this group together, and he's sick of hearing of how Past-Pastor Paul Perfect did it right.

Marvin Music is a creative composer and choir director, but he's inflexible and frequently depressed with the difficult people.

Sister Sally Spiritual knows her Scripture, but the congregation is tired of her dropping a verse onto every passing person.

Joyce Judging is brilliant at the organ and has taken every seminar ever given, but she makes people nervous when she looks them up and down and sighs.

Bob Bossy has everyone impressed and intimidated. He seems to be doing things right, but right is unpopular.

Debbie Depressed keeps coming to church and seeking counsel, but she's no happier now than she was five years ago.

Harriet Hurry's in charge of many committees, but she wears the other members out with her perpetual motion.

Martha Martyr is willing, available, and dutiful, but people are tired of her testimony and tawdry tales and wish she could do one thing without looking for credit.

Larry Lazy is lovable, but he doesn't want to get involved and is critical of those who do.

Winnie Witness is so eager for converts that people flee when they see her coming.

Joe Jock is handsome and athletic, but he's totally absorbed in himself and his body.

Gloria Gossip is friendly to everyone, but what goes in her ear comes out her mouth.

Gilda Guilt is creative, but she's constantly angling for control and is a master manipulator.

Gertrude Grudge has a good memory for details, but if you've ever wronged her, watch out! You are in her book.

How can we ever get along with these difficult people?

How Can We Understand Others?

In my book *Personality Plus,* I analyze the four basic personalities first established by Hippocrates 2,000 years ago. He knew, as I have learned, that we can't deal with people as if they were all the same; it makes life much easier if we learn the strengths and weaknesses of four basic types of people.

For over 30 years I have been studying and using this theory as a tool to understand other people, not to pin labels on people but to open our eyes to their needs and desires. In CLASS—Christian Leaders And Speakers Seminars—we state:

> I must first *know myself*
> So I can *understand others*
> Before I can *help anyone.*

Since the concept of the personalities is the single most important tool for me in getting along with other people, and since I don't know how any marriage holds together without this ability to see each other's strengths and weaknesses objectively, I will give a quick summary of these personalities so you will have a basic understanding of the terms. I have put a reprint of the charts from *Personality Plus* and the Personality Profile in the back of this book for you to use in analyzing yourself and others.

The Popular Personality

The **Sanguines** are the life-of-the-party, colorful, exciting, popular people, with an infectious sense of humor. They have charisma, innate charm, and a magnetic personality. *However,* they may talk too much, can be loose with the facts, want all the attention to be on themselves, seldom follow through on what they start, and don't often achieve their full potential. Their *aim* is to have fun out of life. Their *compulsion* is to turn every event into a party and tell entertaining stories whether or not they happen to be the truth. They usually marry Melancholies to bring order into their lives, and when their mates try to organize them, they rebel.

The Perfect Personality

The **Melancholies** are just the opposite of the Sanguines. They are deep, thoughtful, introspective, phiiosophical, analytical, artistic, and musical. *However,* they focus on the negatives, are very critical of other people, and easily get depressed. Their *aim* is: If it's worth doing, it's worth doing right. Their *compulsion* is to get life, and everyone around them, in perfect order whether or not the others want their lives rearranged. They usually marry Sanguines to lighten and brighten their lives, but when they get them home, they no longer think they're funny and try to get them to be serious and organized.

The Powerful Personality

The **Cholerics** are born leaders. They can organize, motivate, delegate, and stimulate. They exude confidence, like to be busy and can run anything. *However,* they come across as bossy, strong-willed, impetuous and impatient and often become workaholics. They love controversy, manipulate others, and look down on the dummies of life. Their *aim* is: Do it my way now; there is no other way. Their *compulsion* is to right all wrongs and do it quickly. They usually marry Phlegmatics because they are easygoing, agreeable, and relaxed, and then get furious when they won't get out of the chair to move.

The Peaceful Personality

The **Phlegmatics** are the all-purpose people of life, right down the middle, never wanting to cause trouble. They are peaceable, agreeable, patient, and well-balanced, and they have no enemies. *However,* they are often unenthusiastic, indecisive, unmotivated, uninvolved, and indifferent to the plans of others. Their *aim* is: If you have to do it, do it the easy way. They have no real compulsions. They usually marry Cholerics, who obviously have a plan for everyone's life, and then resent it when the Cholerics try to push them into action.

As you practice spotting the basic personality patterns of people, you will be better able to give others what they want in life and to understand them.

• The *Sanguine* wants attention and credit.

• The *Melancholy* wants order and discipline.

• The *Choleric* wants action and obedience.

• The *Phlegmatic* wants peace and quiet.

Now let's apply these principles to the difficult people in the Big Brown Church on the Move.

Chapter 3

How Can We Deal with Difficult People?

How many of you identified with any of the difficult people in the Big Brown Church on the Move? How many of you are strutting and fretting your hour upon the stage with a similar cast?

> Do you perhaps work for Bob Bossy?
> Is your mother-in-law Joyce Judging?
> Do you have a teenage Debbie Depressed?
> Are you running around like Harriet Hurry?
> Are you married to Joe Jock?
> Have you been put under a pile of guilt by Gilda?

All of us can relate to at least one of these characters. They don't bother us as long as we just pass them by at church or at work. We can get along if they exit when we make our entrance. Larry Lazy is easygoing, pleasant, and no trouble at all unless you're the one waiting for him to fix the roof. His wife is sick of hearing how sweet Larry is and how lucky she is to have him. Gertrude Grudge, with her unforgiving spirit and her *Record of Wrongs,* could be funny until you end up in her book.

Difficult people aren't bad from a distance. It's when you have to deal with them personally that you face a dilemma. It's when you're cast in the same drama with them that you pray the show will close. Before we examine these different personalities, we must ask ourselves these questions:

> Do I care enough to make an effort to get along with other people?

Am I willing to find out what they need and give it to them?

Can I maintain a relationship even if the other people don't respond?

Does it really matter what other people think of me?

It will take supernatural desire to put the needs of a difficult person before your own, and it is possible that they may never even notice your noble effort. As Christians, however, we don't have to go it alone. Paul reminds us that the power of the Lord in our life should make a difference. He asks, Does your life in Christ make you strong? Does His love comfort you? Do you have fellowship with the Spirit? Do you feel compassion and love for one another? He continues, "Make me completely happy by having the same thoughts, sharing the same love, and being one in soul and mind. Don't do anything from selfish ambition or from a cheap desire to boast, but be humble toward one another, always considering others better than yourselves. And look out for one another's interests, not just for your own."[3]

Let's approach our getting along with others by using these scriptural principles and caring enough to look out for each other's interests. We should have the mind in us that is also in Christ Jesus.

According to our own background, our spiritual beliefs, and our personality pattern, we develop what we consider a norm for ourselves. We have a feel for what's right and wrong, and people who don't see things our way become difficult. As we learn to deal with other people, we have to realize that just because they're different doesn't make them wrong, but it does make them harder to understand.

Let's look at our fictional characters and see how we can establish a positive relationship with people like them. As we observe the actors in the *Parade of Pious Personalities,* we notice some who are on stage with us, some who are in our play of life. If you don't know any of these people right now, watch out! When the curtain goes up on your life tomorrow, there may be a new member in the cast.

Sam Sermon and Gloria Gossip

Sam Sermon and Gloria Gossip are both Sanguine personalities. They are similar because they love to be on center stage and have leading roles. They each have an engaging sense of humor as well as colorful and appealing personalities. Sam's weaknesses are that he has no sense of timing, he frequently runs out of gas, he's disorganized in his ministry, he speaks off the top of his head, his clothes are loud and sloppy, he can't remember names, and he'll never grow up. Do you know anyone like Sam?

What Does a Person like Sam Need—Besides a Keeper?

Those of you who are not Sanguine think he should just shape up and get his act together, but he's tried and it hasn't worked. He means well, but the organized Melancholies in church can't stand his slapdash manner and his inability to follow a schedule. What does Sam need? He needs help. What kind of help? Quiet help from someone who doesn't need any credit, from someone willing to give without looking for any return on his investment.

How Did Sam Get This Way?

Most Sanguines were adorable children, humorous, impish, and appealing. They got the most attention because they were the most fun. Even the bad things they did were considered cute. As the saying goes, "They got away with murder." They managed to escape responsibility because someone else would always do it for them. In school they were popular and could slide by with a minimum of effort. They knew how to "con others" and make life a bowl of cherries. Some Sanguines can keep this role going throughout life if the supporting cast is very supporting. Women Sanguines tend to get away with this fun approach to life better than men, but in either case the trouble comes when they have to get out and make a serious living.

They have not developed disciplined habits (they've never had to), and they still use their personalities to control difficult situations. Underneath they're insecure because they know, deep inside, that they haven't got what it takes to fulfill the potential everyone has always said they have. When you couple insecurity with a life-of-the-party exterior, you've got trouble. Many Sams are "laughing on the outside, crying on the inside."

How Can We Get Along with an Undisciplined Person like Sam?

Don't criticize him and tell him to improve, even though that seems logical. Sanguines are desperate for praise, and negative words may well paralyze any positive action. Let him know that you really like him, that you think he has a great personality, and that you love to work with him. This should take him off the defensive. Then compliment him on his ability to get along with people and ask how he ever accomplishes so much in a given day.

Sam knows he doesn't get much done, and even though he likes your compliment, he wishes he could finish one day without feeling guilty. He may ask you how he could do this.

At this point, Sam, or any fun-loving Sanguine, is ready for you to offer assistance. If you don't precede the offer with the proper buildup, the Sanguine will refuse help because it's very important that he not lose face or appear incompetent.

Sanguines will love you if you:

- Offer to pick them up and get them somewhere on time—but be prepared for them to be running late, and always call first.

- Take notes for them at meetings, type them up, and give them a copy, always keeping an extra for when they lose what you just gave them.

- Remind them of birthdays and other events. Even better is to buy the card, address and stamp the envelope, and hand it to them to sign before you mail it.

- Put their name on group presents without asking for the money.

- Remember where they hung (or threw) their coats, and when it's time to go, retrieve them.

- Give them little gifts and send cards that are uplifting and humorous.

- Notice any indications of order and congratulate them in hope of promoting some sense of organization.

- Plan surprise gatherings where they are guest of honor.

- Call them before important meetings and remind them what they are supposed to bring.

- Have maps drawn up ahead with directions such as "Watch for big pink house with green shutters. Keep going past the brick church with the columns and then turn right at the Shell station." Never say, "Go north $\frac{2}{10}$ of a mile," as they have no sense of distance and don't like numbers.

Sam and others like him need quiet help done in such a way that he gets the credit. But that's not fair, you say. Right. But if you know a Sam and you do these things, he'll love you for life.

What About Gloria Gossip?

Although she's also a Sanguine, she has a twist to her that differs from Sam's open innocence. She not only loves to talk but she colors her stories up and passes them on in such a way as to give an impression that's not necessarily true. Most people know she exaggerates, but they love to hear her stories.

How Did Gloria Get This Way?

From childhood she had a creative gift for storytelling, and she found she got attention when she had a funny tale to tell. People responded, and she became the life of the party. As a teen she learned she could gain people's confidence if she told them some tidbits about someone else and then pledged them to secrecy. They felt special and somehow obligated to be her friend. Later, when she joined the church, the prayer chain seemed a natural for her talent, followed by spreading information in the church newsletter.

What Is It That Gloria Wants?

She just wants to be popular, and she's found that being the dispenser of deceptive details puts her in the center of the action. Those who need to know come to her.

How Do You Get Along with a Gossip like Gloria?

Much as you may want to, you don't start off by calling her a liar, but you also make sure you don't play her games.

> Don't tell her anything you don't want published.
> Neither give nor listen to "secrets."
> Don't pass on anything she says.
> When she talks about happenings, ask "Were you there?"
> When she tells about people, ask "Have you told them?"

When you have a chance to share with her, say, "You have such an entertaining way of speaking and such a gift for communicating that there's no need for you to exaggerate. Fact is always stranger than fiction." Follow this up with an invitation to do something fun, and let her know you like her for herself. She doesn't need to confide secrets—you like her as she is.

She won't change overnight, but if you're willing to love her for herself and yet not traffic in her gossip, you could help her achieve her potential.

Marvin Music and Gertrude Grudge

Marvin Music and Gertrude Grudge are both Melancholies, although they use their talents differently.

From the time he was a child, Marvin has been musical. He could play "The Train Song" by ear when he was 2½ and moved into the Thompson's Advanced by the time he was six. His whole family is musical, and Marvin was so protected as a prodigy that he was never allowed to go out for sports for fear of hurting a finger. Mother Music and her little notes had a group that rivaled the Von Trapp family, and they have sung in every church of their denomination on the East Coast.

With such talent and background, what's difficult about Marvin? He has a one-track mind and mouth, and he's a perfectionist who gets easily depressed when life isn't perfect.

How Did Marvin Get This Way?

Being brought up in a musical family whose life was spent in church, Marvin knew no other style of living and no other subject of conversation. If it didn't fit on five lines or swing to ¾ time, he wouldn't know what to do with it. He went steady with Missy Melody during college, and they had hoped to make marital music together, but they both got depressed so often that they gave up their attempt at harmony. For a while he tried to tune into Bubbles Beach, but she didn't know *allegro* from Amarillo. Even though she looked great in a bikini, Bubbles messed up everything she touched and thought the *Peer Gynt Suite* was a new brand of chocolates. So Marvin has never married. He keeps to himself in a meticulous condominium with two grand pianos and a well-trained silver poodle. He's lonesome but feels it's better to be alone and right than with company that's wrong.

What Does Marvin Need?

People like Marvin who have one-track lives need others who can at least show interest, if not ability, in their field.

Musical Melancholies love harmony and balance in life. They are very analytical and deep, and they want to define their terms.

At one of our marriage seminars, Fred decided to survey what percentage of the Melancholies were musical. He asked a neatly dressed man heading into the Melancholy group to count up how many of the Melancholies were musical. It seemed like a simple request.

Had we asked a Sanguine, she would have gone into her group and said, "How many of you are musical?" (If she remembered to do it at all.) They would all have raised their hands because Sanguines always want to be whatever seems to be popular today, and they all know how to find music on a radio. A Choleric would have made a quick and realistic accounting and proceeded with the other items of business. A Phlegmatic would have asked, but even musical Phlegmatics wouldn't raise their hands for fear the question would lead them into some involvement or require them to join something. So what did the Melancholies do?

When the meticulous man returned, he came forward with his clipboard and a lengthy report. "Fred asked me to see how many people in our group were musical. I asked the question, and no one responded. They were thinking. After a while one said, 'How do you define musical?' That brought a murmur of mutual concern. 'Is musical someone who plays an instrument or someone who appreciates music?' We discussed this for a while and decided we needed to make two counts: one for those who played instruments and one for those with appreciation for music. I then asked for all those who played to raise their hands. As I counted, a lady asked, 'How about if you used to play the piano when you were a child?' We talked it over and accepted her. Then a man asked, 'What if you're going to start guitar lessons next week?' We let him in and made three counts: Past, present, and future. Next I questioned, 'How many of you appreciate music?' A young lady asked, 'What kind?' We finally divided our question into three sections: classical, contemporary, and gospel. I've added up all the totals in our six-part report, and here it is."

He then read his complicated six-part report, three columns of the past, present, and future of those who play instruments and three columns of types: classical, contemporary, or gospel. This made six subtotals plus a grand total, far more than Fred had ever expected. The results showed that all but a few of the Melancholies were musical in some sense and that they were detail-conscious and perfectionists.

What do these serious people really want? People who are like them or who show sympathetic interest in their chosen field. If you find their subject of interest, they will be glad to converse; if you don't, they won't bring it up but will sit quietly, assuming that no one there is very bright and no one cares about them.

What do Melancholies *not* want? Anyone who upsets their systematic way of life or who suggests that they throw caution to the wind and just have a good time.

The Melancholies have difficulty in choosing a mate because they want a perfect person, and there aren't any. When they find someone like them and each is looking for perfection, it makes the test twice as hard. The few couples I know who are both Melancholies get along well on details, housekeeping, and creativity, but when they both get depressed at the same time it is unbearable.

When the Melancholy is attracted by nature to his opposite, a cheerful but disorganized Sanguine, he spends his life weighing whether the joy is worth the chaos that goes with it.

In either case someone like Marvin, a talented perfectionist, will never find that perfect mate and may have to settle for second-best and be depressed about it.

How Do We Deal with People like Marvin Music?

Hold to their order and organization. Just knowing what people want in life by having even a limited understanding of their personalities makes getting along with them so much easier. If they want *order and organization,* then let's try to give it to them. If we know they get nervous when there's no schedule or it's being ignored, then we could be the one to pull things together.

If they ever ask us how they could change for the better (and even then proceed with caution), you might suggest an attempt at flexibility. We have several Melancholies on the CLASS staff, and I've been the cause of their learning how to be flexible.

One day Barbara asked me for the morning's schedule, and I replied, "There isn't one. You're going to learn to be flexible."

She softly said, "If I don't know the schedule, how can I be flexible?"

Lead into their pet topics. Since the Melancholies are not people-oriented and have difficulty feeling at ease at social functions, you will be their friend for life if you can rescue them from a lonely corner and ask about their area of expertise. You can be sure they have one, so ask a few leading questions. They tend to give simple answers until you hit their pet topic.

My son-in-law is an expert on the hand-signed paper money of General Chinese Gordon done during the Sudanese siege of Khartoum. This is not a hot topic at social events, but when I throw the conversation to him, people are fascinated at the historical tales he has to tell.

A Melancholy like Marvin will never forget you if you've cared enough to find out what's dear to his heart and given him an opportunity to share.

Realize how easily they get depressed. For those of us who don't often get depressed, it's hard to realize the types of slights that can throw a Melancholy into a negative state. For example:

- Positive comments made quietly across the room may be assumed to be negative.

- Any statement of "You look great today" makes them wonder what was wrong with them yesterday.

- Joking about them in any vein will probably be taken seriously. "You may think that was funny, but I took it as a direct insult."

Because Melancholies are deep and serious, they take even light thoughts and turn them into heavy truths. Watch your tongue and don't be the one to ruin their Christmas.

How Did Gertrude Grudge Get This Way?

Gertrude Grudge, like Marvin Music, is a very talented and intelligent person who was no doubt a child prodigy. Right from her early years, Gertrude found that people did not appreciate her abilities and that she was not treated fairly. Because of her retentive and organized mind, Gertrude began to keep notes of personal injustices which have grown into her *Record of Wrongs*. Because she can validate every personal clash to have been caused by the other person, she has no concept that any fault lies with her. She does not forgive because these people have been wrong and they don't deserve to be let off the hook.

In school other kids got the prizes she deserved. At work the bosses have all been unfair and played favorites with the cute and brainless. In marriage her husband is inferior and her children unappreciative. How Did Gertrude Grudge get this way? She's taken note of hurts from the very beginning and has learned that when you expect the worst you'll usually get it.

What Is She Looking For?

Someone who'll agree with her that life is unfair and that the wicked do prosper. She will go over her current list with anyone who'll listen, and because way underneath her conscience tells her there must be one decent person somewhere, she needs constant validation that her *Record of Wrongs* is *right!* She'll say, "I'll never forgive the pastor for making fun of me at choir practice." Even though you were there and know that Sam Sermon was only being humorous, what she wants you to do is affirm that her judgment was correct and that you would hate him too if you were in her shoes. Obviously, if you agree you may be quoted as she reads her book to the next victim.

How Can You Get Along with Gertrude Grudge?

There are three approaches to getting along with a bitter and unforgiving person like Gertrude.

   1. Agree with her.

   2. Try to change her opinion now and then.

   3. Avoid her at all costs.

The third approach is the only sure-fire way to deal with Gertrude. Many people before you have chosen this path as the only hope for self-preservation. That's why Gertrude is so lonely and in need of friends.

That's why she has people over to her house after church but few reciprocate. Gertrude doesn't realize that people can see her *Record of Wrongs* (even when she doesn't carry it) as the root of bitterness that springs up in her countenance and that can be seen in her scowl from the choir loft.

If you choose to buck the tide and befriend Gertrude, you need only agree with her that Bob Bossy is out to get her off the board, that Gloria Gossip should have her lips stitched together, that Debbie Depressed needs a psychiatrist, and that your own mother has a big mouth. If you can go along with this approach, you will be accepted, but please remember that you, by having nodded your head, will now have said all the things Gertrude has reviewed. Playing with Gertrude is a dangerous game.

Could you try to straighten her out? Yes, you could try. No doubt others have tried before you. Where are the others who've tried? Depressed, distraught, departed, or dead! Gertrude does not take kindly to those who have implied that she is harsh, critical, or judgmental. They have been given a whole page in her book and their sins repeated to all who will listen. Many well-meaning parishioners have fled the church when they found themselves on Gertrude's blacklist.

What can we do with Gertrude? Smile? Nod? Stay uninvolved? If you do somehow get into a reviewing stand with Gertrude and she pours out negatives about one of her cases, kindly and quietly point out that you don't agree and that you feel she should look at their good qualities. This will keep you from being quoted and might give her cause for reflection. If she responds positively to your suggestion, you will know that God has personally appointed you to lead her into the paths of righteousness for His name's sake.

In any case, do pray for the Gertrudes in your life. They're hurt and lonely and have no idea why!

Bob Bossy and Harriet Hurry

Bob Bossy and Harriet Hurry are both Cholerics. They are born leaders, dynamic and active, and can run anything. They both charge in where angels fear to tread, and they both exude confidence. These are all exceptional qualities, but somehow both Bob and Harriet intimidate other people, who feel insecure in their presence.

What Do Bob and Harriet Want in Life?

They both need a feeling of control, a need to be in charge. Rarely do two such people marry each other, since they need to bring in a resident conformist who will follow their lead. People like them are frequently workaholics because they must be sure to stay on top of whatever they're doing, and they like work better than people. They have compulsions to change things and right the wrongs of life.

How Did Bob Get This Way?

The Choleric personality is the easiest to spot in children because Cholerics start very young to get things under their control. One lady recently told me at the end of a Personality Plus seminar, "My son started controlling me when he was only three months old. He would be lying in his infant seat and I would pick the seat up and move him to another room. He would scream. No matter what I tried, it didn't work. Finally I'd put him back where he'd been before and he'd smile. This happened so many times that when he screamed I'd rush him back to where he'd been. He's been controlling us ever since."

Cholerics are born with an urge to take charge, and as they grow up they run everything they touch. They usually excel, usually win, and usually are right. This pattern puts them out in front but doesn't lead to popularity. As they become aware that their peers don't flock around them, they make work their god and don't worry about people. They aim for the top in whatever profession they choose. Many become doctors, lawyers, and company presidents. They chafe under anyone else's authority and prefer to be in business for themselves.

Bob has become a doctor. He owns a Mercedes and thinks rules are for other people. When asked to be chairman of the board, he took over gladly because he had already noticed how poorly the "dummies" were doing. He assumed that people who weren't efficient would naturally want to improve, and so he instantly organized the church board in a logical manner. Bob was right about their need but wrong in assuming people wanted to change, even for the better. He learned the plight of the eager Choleric: Right is not always popular.

How Can We Get Along with a Bossy Person like Bob?

If you really want to get along, there is one obvious answer: *Do it their way now!* Cholerics do not need the praise that Sanguines crave; they only want obedience. They will, however, take a difference of opinion as a rejection of them and their ideas. This feeling won't devastate them as it would a Melancholy because they have learned over the years that they don't need people. They can slough off what might hurt others by telling themselves the other person doesn't know anything anyway. Don't waste time pouting or withdrawing in hope they'll notice and come begging for forgiveness; they dislike weakness and will turn away from tears.

Don't expect them to notice their own failings. Repeatedly, as I do Personality Plus seminars, I have the Bobs and Harriets completing their Personality Profiles, then looking up and saying, "I have most of the strengths but none of the weaknesses." One lady who had done the test without reading the directions had checked every single strength and only one weakness. In the margin she had written by the one weakness "only sometimes."

Recently a doctor like Bob Bossy showed me his test and said, "There's no way I can check any of these weaknesses. I don't have any." Later in the evening as I chatted with him, he admitted he did have one problem: "I always seem to hire weak, sniveling nurses. When I walked in yesterday, they all started to cry and huddle together. I asked them what terrible thing had happened, and they said they were afraid of me. Can you imagine that?! I straightened them out and reminded them that if they would just do what I told them to do when I told them to do it, they wouldn't have anything to be afraid of."

In his mind he had taken care of the problem, and he wanted my insight as to why he seemed to consistently hire "weak, sniveling nurses." He had absolutely no idea that even part of the problem could be with him.

Avoid the appearance of mutiny. Since the Choleric must be the master of his fate, "the captain of his soul,"[4] he will take harsh measures upon anyone who tries to scuttle his ship, whether his ship is the business, the church, or the family. Since power is the Choleric's need, any rumblings which might go unnoticed by other Personalities may be perceived as a threat to his authority. I have seen this scenario often in Christian circles. The Choleric has developed his ministry at church and has brought in a sharp assistant, but then he gets word that this person he has "trusted" has gotten "a little too big for his britches"—so he has to go. Unsuspecting individuals without this understanding don't realize that being too good, too bright, or too promising can scuttle their own ship when a Choleric is captain.

We all want to do our best, but in working with a Bob Bossy, don't charge ahead without checking your ideas and helping him to think that the new thought has sprung from his mind.

"That which in the captain is but a Choleric word, in the soldier is flat blasphemy."[5]

Realize that they are master manipulators. People like Bob Bossy have spent years doing the right things for the right people who sit in the right places. They have built debts for others so that at any time they may "call in their markers." While this ability impresses many people, and these obligations are often used for good purposes, it is well to be aware of these Choleric tricks so that you won't be surprised when your chips are cashed in without notice.

Confront them if necessary. If you are living or working with an extreme Choleric, one who never lets anyone else express an opinion, you may have to confront this person for your own sanity. Realize that they look down on weakness and respect strength, so if a Choleric is pushing you around, he probably thinks you're pushable.

If this strong personality is your mate, don't set out to pick a fight but decide what issue bothers you the most and make a test case of it. Since Cholerics want everything to be right, you might start by asking, "Do you realize I have been very unhappy lately?"

"Unhappy? Why?"

"Because I've realized I never have an opportunity to share my opinion on any subject with you."

"What do you mean? I always let you talk!"

It's at this point that most of us quit in our effort. But keep trying: "I know you *feel* you do, but I feel frustrated and I'd like to share my thoughts with you when you have time."

When I've approached Fred this way, he's almost always taken the time. Recently I told him there was one thing I wanted to discuss when he had time. He sat right down and I expressed my feelings. I let him know how much I appreciated his compliments on my speaking and other activities but that I didn't like his "however" clauses. He had no idea what I meant but wanted to know immediately what he was doing wrong with his well-meaning compliments.

I explained how he ended each "you did well" with a "however, when you do that again...." I told him that I would be thrilled if half the time he could praise me without an accompanying suggestion for how I could do it better.

He had no idea he did this and asked me to please stop him the next time he did it. He hasn't done it since.

Cholerics want to be perfect and will change quickly if approached positively. Sometimes we bottle up what bothers us and then explode over some triviality. This outburst shows the other person how unstable we are and almost never has a positive effect.

How Did Harriet Hurry Get This Way?

Usually the person who's running from place to place and who is feverishly involved is covering up for the fact that she has some deep insecurities she doesn't wish to face. Perpetual action keeps her from that dreaded moment when she finds herself alone with herself and doesn't like the real person she sees in the mirror. She also may have a distressing home situation that she's running away from: an alcoholic husband, a teen on drugs, an elderly parent. She usually keeps this well-covered and appears to be in excellent control of each committee. Her life may well be empty, and even while surrounded with people she may be lonely. Watch for possible signs of hidden sadness in the eyes of busy people.

How Do You Handle Harriet?

Try to become her friend. It will take effort and planning to get acquainted with Harriet because she's so busy, but find a way and ask her some introspective questions. Encourage her to tell of her childhood or her current home situation. Remember, she doesn't wish to exhibit weakness and may not let you get too close, but as you sense this you will catch a glimpse of the desperate need she has down inside.

In counseling CLASS members, usually exceptional women, I find that many (like Harriet) have built strong denial systems. Because of their Choleric personalities, they have perhaps hidden some childhood trauma from everyone in their life. They have put it in a box and buried the experience. They may be in the process of burying a disappointing marriage or a difficult relationship so they can stay strong.

One very powerful lady who came to CLASS was a typical Harriet who ran everything in her church and town. When it was time to go to her small group, where interaction was expected, she refused to go. She was afraid of a place where *she might be vulnerable* or transparent. She was also, as with most Cholerics, unwilling to enter a situation where *she wasn't in control.* Vulnerability and lack of control are two great fears of these fearless people, and when you understand these hidden concerns, you will be able to help such Cholerics.

On the third day of CLASS, I found a very large lady standing in the corner of the hall. Tears were streaming down her face. When I asked her what was wrong, she said, "Nothing—I'm very strong."

Cholerics must appear strong at all times.

"But you're crying," I countered. She burst into tears, and I led her to a counselor, who found she had an unbearable home situation with a husband who was not working but criticizing how she was making the living. She was ready to scream.

She had looked so under control, so in charge, so much the captain of her soul, that people had shied away from her. Yet here she was in desperate need of someone in whose presence she dared to be weak, vulnerable, and out of control. She needed help, but she didn't want to expose the chink in her armor.

Don't make hasty judgments. When you think of the strong woman who runs everything, realize that this may be a cover-up. Don't toss her to the winds too quickly. The person who never has a problem to share may have the biggest problem of all. You may be the only one who has the genuine concern to really find out what's going on underneath the confident exterior.

Let her work. People who are not workaholics can't imagine that some people are only happy when working. They don't want to sit down, and they don't want to watch TV; they want to be achieving something all the time. Once we accept this perpetual motion, whether we understand it or not, we can relax and let them work.

When I was first married and my wonder-woman mother-in-law came to visit, I was hurt, sometimes even insulted, when she would take my stove apart and use steel wool to shine up every rod on my oven racks. I took it as a personal slap at my housekeeping abilities, so when I knew she was coming I'd clean everything in sight so she wouldn't find one negligent corner.

One winter day after I had scoured everything, I left her in my home while I went to a necessary meeting. When I came back she met me at the door in yellow rubber gloves, and I couldn't imagine what she'd found to scrub. She proudly took me to the kitchen, where she had laid out on the counters three old rubber rafts that had been deflated and resting in a corner of the patio for the season. She had found them, seen that they were dusty and cobwebbed, blown them up, and scrubbed them clean!

That extreme experience taught me that she was going to work no matter what. I realized that her self-worth was tied up in how much she could achieve, and that when she sat around as a guest she felt useless. Once I understood that her compulsive cleaning of my house was not an insult but a necessity for feeling good about herself, I was able to relax and let her work. I stopped excessive cleaning before she came and let her go to it. Once she polished my oven so well that I opened the door, letting the light reflect on the gleaming sides, and placed a philodendron on the shelf. This display became the focal point of the kitchen, and as each member of the family returned that night, he or she noticed the shining stove with the spotlighted leaves cascading over the ovenracks.

If the shoemaker elves want to stay up all night and make shoes, let them do it. Then be sure to appreciate all the new shoes they give you.

Know that he/she means well. People like Bob and Harriet who can run things tend to rise to the top in church and social functions for two reasons:

> No one else wants the job.
> They know they can do it better than anyone else.

They don't necessarily seek to be president, but people put them there and then wonder why they're running everything. You've heard the old saying, "If you want a job done, give it to a busy person."

Bob and Harriet mean well and work hard, yet they are frequently ostracized by other people who look at them as power-hungry. Don't be the kind of person who looks for a Choleric to take charge and then is critical when he does.

Larry Lazy

In contrast to Gertrude Grudge and her *Record of Wrongs,* Larry loves everyone and everyone loves him. He's a middle-of-the-road, all-purpose, inoffensive person. Churches have special halos for people like Larry. Chatty Sanguines love them because they listen. Controlling Cholerics surround themselves with them because they'll agree to anything. Moody Melancholies appreciate how they adjust to whatever mood you're in today. Phlegmatics are popular in the parish, so what kind of problems could you possibly have with such passive people?

They tend to avoid responsibility, lack enthusiasm for new projects, arrive late and criticize those who take action. They don't feel these are really weaknesses but good judgment. They know better than to assume responsibility for something they shouldn't be doing. Some projects aren't worthy of enthusiasm, and some people are too pushy.

Even though these low-key people dampen others' initiative, they do bring balance to aggressive groups and families. Cyndi, a dynamic Sanguine-Choleric, describes her Phlegmatic husband this way: "I picture him standing on a hill holding the strings to my balloons. I'm flying high with many different colorful projects floating off in diverse directions. When I've got too many balloons going too far, he calmly pulls in my strings and brings me back to earth."

Yes, the Phlegmatic is the great leveler of life.

How Did Larry Get This Way?

Don't we all wish we had this easygoing, well-liked nature? The Phlegmatic is born that way and finds it easier to stay out of trouble than to take a chance of getting into it. This avoidance does keep him from being adventurous or having ardent passions over any person or plan.

In growing up, Phlegmatics find that being average is good enough, but often because they are so amiable they are thrust into positions of leadership. It must have been about Phlegmatics that Shakespeare wrote, "Some are born great, some achieve greatness, and some have greatness thrust upon them."[6]

What Problems Will You Have with Larry Lazy?

Realize that he won't get enthused. Cholerics and Phlegmatics usually get attracted to one another and then live to regret the relationship. The Choleric becomes the cheerleader, trying endlessly to get the Phlegmatic to let out a rousing cheer. The Choleric expects that the docile Phlegmatic will perk up under his leadership and then is dumbfounded when no measure of enthusiasm will excite his neutral nature. Instead of improving, the

Phlegmatic tends to be so overwhelmed in the presence of strong-willed people that he or she retreats and lets the others do it.

My daughter Lauren, a Choleric, once was a co-teacher with a Phlegmatic in a Sunday school class. As they would meet to prepare, the Phlegmatic never got enthused over any of the lesson material. She had no input or suggestions, wouldn't teach the lesson herself, and gave no words of praise once Lauren had successfully taught the lesson. If you are in such a relationship and want to get along without frustration, you have to realize that the Phlegmatic won't get enthused and may criticize what you do.

If you need excitement and encouragement, you won't get it from this Larry Lazy.

Understand that he'll avoid responsibility. If you find yourself chairman of a committee with Phlegmatics, you will soon learn that they need more motivation than the other personalities. They'll listen and agree with the principles but won't want to make them happen enough to get to work. While you may be able to see through a large list to the goal ahead, Larry Lazy only wants to deal with one item at a time, if that.

One day in a gift shop, I heard a lady yell out at her Phlegmatic husband, "I've been the guidance counselor of this family for 30 years! *You* make this decision. I resign!" She stormed out of the store and left a stunned man stranded among the straw baskets.

Know that Phlegmatics hide problems. Because they don't like to deal with difficulties, Phlegmatics hide their problems like Easter eggs. When someone like Larry Lazy finds himself holding a basket of problems, he decides the best way to get rid of them is to hide them. He puts some in the branches of the trees too high for anyone to see, some behind logs where you'd have to trip to find them, and some under rocks where the weight will hopefully flatten them into obscurity. This hiding of the eggs of trouble suits the Phlegmatic's "out of sight, out of mind" mentality and works until other people come along. The curious Sanguine stares up and cries out, "Look at those troubles up there in the tree! I wonder what will happen if I shake the branches? Why, here they lie, all smashed before me, the scrambled eggs of trouble!"

The Melancholy looks down as he wanders through the woods and sees old Easter eggs behind the logs spoiling in the summer sun. "Why, I thought these troubles had been gathered up and dealt with long ago. This is so depressing! What can we ever do with them now?" The Choleric, with his compulsive need to right all wrongs, charges forth, kicking over every rock he sees. As he finds that the Phlegmatic has hidden all the problems, he vows, "That dummy! I'll never let him handle any of my eggs again."

If you want problems solved, don't hand the basket to Larry Lazy.

How Do You Deal with Phlegmatics?

Contrary to the difficult natures of other people, Phlegmatics provide a placid plateau without problems. Once you accept that they won't get excited and they will flee from controversy, you'll have no troubles in getting along. If you are courageous, you may try to challenge and motivate them to action, but frequently they'll feel that it's just too much like work. They mean well, but they have learned that if they can procrastinate long enough, someone else will do it.

How Do You Motivate Them?

Since my daughter Lauren is a Choleric married to a Phlegmatic, she has had to do one of three things:

1. Do it herself.
2. Hire someone else to do it.
3. Find a way to move her husband to action.

Lauren needed a new floodlight bulb over the barbecue. She asked Randy to put one in, and he happily agreed to do it. Phlegmatics are always agreeable, but you can't count on performance.

As weeks went by, Lauren bought the bulb and set it on the top of the stepladder directly under the socket. One dark night she assigned Randy to cook a steak on the barbecue, and he headed out. Soon he returned and said, "I can't see out there!"—as if that was news to Lauren. She showed him the ladder, and because she had prepared his way, he finally put in the bulb.

As I shared this story in a seminar, a lady told me she had done the same thing, but her Phlegmatic husband got a flashlight and had her hold it over the barbecue rather than climb up and put in the bulb.

Lauren and Randy have agreed that she will make a list of what Randy needs to do at home and put a completion date next to each item. As long as the list isn't overwhelming, he does the work and smiles with pride when he can cross off a job well done. It takes creative motivation to move a Larry Lazy!

Sally Spiritual

When Sally Spiritual takes the Personality Profile, she comes out Choleric-Phlegmatic, an unnatural and unlikely combination. Her Choleric is obvious: She carries the keys to the kingdom, automatically putting every cabinet and closet under her firm control; she gives tours of the church facility; she's never done anything wrong and has the Scripture to prove it.

How does she appear Phlegmatic even to herself? Many Cholerics, when not in charge of a situation, pull back and appear Phlegmatic. Some, as in my case, happened to marry another Choleric and found that two functioning Cholerics in one family was one too many. When two Cholerics are together in family or business, one of three things happens:

1. They both agree and charge forth toward a united goal.
2. They fight for control.
3. One pulls back and plays Phlegmatic.

In retrospect, number 3 is what I did. Even though I didn't understand the personalities at the time, I found that I couldn't control Fred. I didn't often agree but I didn't dare fight (he was bigger and had the money), so I played submissive. "Yes, Fred. Whatever you want, Fred."

Had I taken the profile at that time, I would have been an odd mix of Choleric-Phlegmatic: Choleric when out in the world, where I was president of everything, and Phlegmatic when I was home with Fred.

How Did Sally Get This Way?

Sally probably had a strong Choleric parent who always appeared to be in control and who carried a ring of keys denoting authority. Sally saw from childhood that to get one's way, one first should get the keys. Since Sally was brought up "in the church," she learned that church was to be one's first priority. Sally learned all the verses and has a great urge to let everyone know what she knows. She is somewhat legalistic about the laws of life, and her children tend to stay away from church.

Her other parent was probably Phlegmatic, and Sally learned from that one how to pull back when the odds were overwhelming, and to appear not to care how the whole issue came out.

What Does Sally Want from Others?

She wants to be known as a good church person, a spiritual giant with a verse for all seasons and reasons, and she wants to hear people praise her dedication. She likes to have people need to come to her to get the keys to any cabinet. She wants to feel that if something ever happened to her, the whole church would collapse. She's willing to do all the work if only the people will appreciate her sacrifice.

How Did Other Choleric-Phlegmatic Persons Get This Way?

Since this combination is not a natural one, part of it is a survival act. If the person is basically Choleric (like me), he may masquerade as a Phlegmatic in certain situations, such as home, work, or church, where trying to be in charge would lead to disaster. One lady at CLASS told me she was this split, and when I questioned her I found she had a Choleric husband whom she knew better than to challenge at home. At work, however, she ran a large county office where her word was law. She had a split aggressive-submissive personality, although she was in no way mentally ill. She had learned that to get along she had to be two different people.

Sometimes this unlikely split is just the opposite: The nature is Phlegmatic, but the person is forced by his position at work to assume what appear to be Choleric traits. The Phlegmatic is very adaptable, and when properly motivated by money or threat of death, he can produce what appears to be a Choleric result. It is possible that he may be a real Phlegmatic at work, and for a time, if the Choleric mate at home is ill or absent, he assumes an unnatural leadership role and appears to be Choleric.

Usually this Choleric-Phlegmatic split is evidence that one of these patterns is true and the other is a learned response to life.

How Can I Deal with Them?

Ask enough questions to find out which is the person's natural personality and which is his/her learned response to life. As you determine this, you will be able to follow the behavior guidelines to that personality. If the situation or friendship is favorable, you might share these truths with the individual.

In these unnatural splits, we find that the person has been wondering for years who he really is.

Remember, if we don't know who we are ourselves, it's difficult to understand or help anyone else.

If the Phlegmatic is the natural personality pattern, know that the individual would prefer to "let George do it." The Phlegmatic who has been forced to be in charge against his natural inclinations will pull back whenever possible and will resent being pushed into leadership. He will, however, be a balanced and purposeful person when gently moved into a leadership position.

If the Choleric is the natural trait, know that the individual is uncomfortable when not in control. As we recognize the need for the strong man or woman to be in control, we can easily see why he or she may appear to have a split personality. Marita once dated a suave continental millionaire. He was gracious, charming, and in control. When he took our family out to dinner, we always went to a place where everyone knew him and greeted him by name. We would receive the red-carpet treatment. For dinner favors he would give out gold Cross pens and flowers for the ladies.

Once we had him to our home at Christmastime. He came late and brought presents but seemed ill-at-ease and would not sit down with the rest of us. He seemed to have lost his strong personality, and our uncertainty toward his bizarre behavior made us all uncomfortable. The next time we saw him, it was on his own turf, and he was himself again. Then we all realized that he only knew how to function where he was in control in his own comfort zone. When not in charge, he withdrew and appeared to be Phlegmatic.

Usually the Choleric-Phlegmatic combination is functional more than natural: One is a basic pattern while the other is a survival kit to salvage the situations of life.

Debbie Depressed

Debbie Depressed is no doubt a charter member of an organization called The Greater Grouches of America, catering to that select group of people who were "born in a bad mood." Members receive a button and a parchment membership certificate that "gives them a license to grumble, put down, hack off, and generally express grouchy attitudes."[7]

If there is one kind of person who is the least favorite of all, it is the grumbling, complaining, depressed grouch—the one who is never happy over anything, the one who murmurs and disputes like the Hebrews in the desert, the one who complains that "no one ever thinks of poor little me," the one who owns his own resident black cloud that hovers over him and casts a chill on all those around him.

Do you know anyone like this? There must be many if there is a national organization for those "born in a bad mood."

How Did They Get This Way?

Were they really born in a bad mood? My 30-year study of personalities shows me that we are all born with certain strengths and weaknesses and that some people really are born in a bad mood. They are usually Melancholy-Phlegmatic combinations who are easily depressed and not motivated to do much about it. Their response to the issues of life is frequently negative, and their assessment of any situation will bring about complaints.

Because they were born with a pessimistic nature, they saw the worst in things as children and picked up negative comments like a magnet. Statements that would have bounced off a Sanguine were sucked in, swallowed up, and digested, giving permanent symptoms of distress.

We find in CLASS that people of this Melancholy-Phlegmatic combination have a history of rejections, many of them real and some imagined:

> Their mother didn't love them.
> Their father wanted a boy.
> Their brothers were the favorites.
> The older siblings got the privileges.
> The younger ones got the attention.
> Teachers never liked them.
> Recess was a ground of rejection.
> No one wanted them on the team.
> The pastor avoids meeting with them.
> Their mate finds other people more appealing.
> They don't get invited to parties.
> The doctors can't find anything really wrong
> and on and on.

Is it any wonder that we have difficulty in dealing with the Debbie Depresseds of life?

What Do Depressed People Want?

Those of us who are happy assume that depressed people want to be happy like us. We try to jolly them up and say, "Life isn't that bad. Look at the bright side of things." But they can't cheer up so easily, and that inability gets them more depressed. They review in their minds all those people who have rejected them in the past and assume that you will do the same. They know they aren't normal, that nobody cares, and that they'd be better off dead. So what do they want?

> Improved circumstances.
> A friend who won't reject them.
> The assurance that they aren't crazy.
> A reason for living.

So what can you do about it? The average person avoids depressed people and stays away from those who are born in a bad mood, but if you're up to the challenge, here are some suggestions.

How Can We Get Along with Debbie Depressed?

Expect rejection. Few people make the effort to help the depressed because they sense from the beginning that their advances will be turned down. Part of the pattern of depression is the belief that no one really cares, and so when someone appears to like them, they're looked upon with suspicion. "What are they trying to get out of me?" is a question that runs through the disturbed mind. Many people quit trying to help at this point, reinforcing the fear that no one will ever care.

If we are looking to receive something from this type of relationship, we will be disappointed, but if we are willing to give sacrificially, expecting nothing in return, we can get along with Debbie. If we expect rejection, which is Debbie's way of getting back at all those who have hurt her, then we won't be done in by it, won't take it personally, and will be able to go on to the next level.

Be a real friend. When you picture that Debbie's lifelong experience has been one of real or imagined rejection, you can see why she has built a wall around herself and won't let anyone in. If you come on too strong, she'll push you aside. If you appear too happy, you'll turn her off. If you're discouraged over your own life, you'll make her more depressed. What's left for you to be? Debbie and other depressed people need a real friend who will be understanding and compassionate, who won't scold, laugh loudly, or put her down.

If she's in your church, let her know when functions of interest are held, and volunteer to pick her up. Try to match her excuses with answers such as "I can get you a babysitter," or "I'll stay right with you," or "It's a small group and they won't call on you to pray."

If she's a co-worker, encourage her. Notice any progress and comment sincerely. Don't let people pick on her or make fun of her.

If she's a relative, keep her moving and don't let her withdraw from people and reality. Encourage her to get counsel from some objective person.

If she's your child, take her to some quiet place, promise you won't interrupt, and then ask her how she really feels about life. In a recent survey, more than 50 percent of the teens questioned said they believe we will all be killed by drugs or terrorists and there's not much we can do about it. No wonder they have so little hope!

Give hope. Shakespeare said, "The miserable have no other medicine, but only hope."[8] Since the depressed person often thinks he's crazy and there's no reason to keep living, you will serve God's purpose if you can be the one to give hope. Share past problems of a similar nature and show how you have been able to learn from your experience. Let the person know that other people have had similar pressures and survived, that we can "rejoice in hope of the glory of God." Show that we as Christian believers don't sorrow as those who have no hope, but that God uses our depressions and trials for ultimate good: "We glory in tribulations also: knowing that tribulation worketh patience; and patience, experience; and experience, *hope.*"[9]

In CLASS our aim is to teach others how to give hope. In each one of our lives, there is some experience where we have gained victory that will give that ray of hope to others.[10]

Carolyn wrote me: "Thank you for the special way you have helped me to realize that with God all things are possible. Two weeks ago I spoke to over 200 women at the Sanger Christian Brunch and experienced what to me was a miracle. Before attending CLASS I had no thought of ever being able to speak, let alone what I might have to share that would give *hope* to others. However, I've learned that through prayer, preparation, and practice God is able to work through me in showing others how to forgive people who have misused or abused them in the past."

So many depressed people are still clinging to the hurts of the past, as Gertrude Grudge and Debbie Depressed each do. Carolyn explained how women she had known for years told her for the first time some of the traumas and abuses they had lived through in the past. Some were still suffering from the experience and were comforted by Carolyn's message of hope.

Help set realistic goals. A person who is seriously depressed functions emotionally at about a third-grade level. Knowing this will keep you from expecting too much. Until Debbie improves, it is wise to help her set realistic goals, things she can achieve without risk of failure. Have her choose where to go for lunch versus having her over to your house. Let her bring the rolls to a potluck supper versus making turkey tetrazzini. Help her organize a daily planner versus setting goals for the next two years. Give her a hand with some spring cleaning versus telling her that Saturday would be a good day for her to clean the house.

Discuss possible alternatives. Frequently, depressed people want their circumstances improved but are too disturbed to see clear alternatives. Don't assume that they have analyzed all possibilities. Ask what would be ideal circumstances if they had their way, and then see how close that is to reality. Sometimes just opening up a chance for the future can give hope.

Some Debbies are perpetual counsel-seekers. They've worn the pastor out, and now they throw their depression on every visiting evangelist or speaker. They go to the ladies' Bible study and drain the teacher with their tales of woe. Everyone could give them the same accurate advice, but they still wouldn't change. They are happy with misery and the attention it gets them, and they have no intention of taking steps to improve.

If you have a Debbie draining you, give some kind of an assignment and tell her you can't see her again until she's done this. If she's serious and wants your friendship, she'll make an effort. If she is only asking for attention, she won't do it and you may not see her on your doorstep again.

A word of caution: A person like Debbie can easily attach herself to a strong friend who is willing to care for her. She can pull the life from you, make you feel guilty if you go anywhere without her, and never seem to improve. Unfortunately, if this happens, and you have to extricate yourself from the relationship, she then validates in her mind that everyone rejects her.

For those interested in further study on the subject of depression, please read my book *Blow Away the Black Clouds.*

Joyce Judging and Gilda Guilt

Joyce and Gilda are complementary blends of Choleric and Melancholy. Joyce is a Choleric: strong, outgoing, and in control, but also judgmental, scornful, and nagging. She also has some Melancholy traits: She's studious, teachable, and analytical, but she remembers wrongs, is depressed at home, and has standards beyond anyone's ability.

Gilda is Melancholy: sacrificial, creative, and persistent, but also guilty of remembering wrongs, instilling guilt, and being hard to please. She also has some Choleric traits: She is strong-willed, goal-oriented, and in charge, but also manipulative, demanding, and possessive.

The Choleric-Melancholy combination is the most powerful of all. The Choleric part wants control, and the Melancholy is willing to stay with it until it is accomplished perfectly. These people have the greatest potential for leadership and accomplishment but also a subtle and insidious way of bending people to their own will.

When I look at the totals on the Personality Profile and see a person with a somewhat even Choleric and Melancholy split, I can assume I have someone who is constantly molding people into his own image, someone who is never content with things or people as they are. Such people can just look at a person and make him feel insecure and incompetent. They have excellent judgmental abilities, and their conclusions are usually correct but often inconsiderate.

I have observed so many men who are Choleric-Melancholy who have married Sanguine women and set about to remake them. Because they are so strong, determined, and manipulative, the Choleric-Melancholy man can in fact beat the frivolous, fun-loving Sanguine to a point where she's not sure who she is.

When I find a score where the man is Choleric-Melancholy and the wife is Sanguine-Melancholy (an unnatural blend and usually a depressed Sanguine), I can take a calculated guess that we have a wife who has been remade. I recently asked one man of this pattern what traits his wife had when he married her that he didn't like. He gave me a quick list. "What did you do about these faults?" I asked.

"I beat them out of her," was his reply.

"What's she like now?"

"She's not much fun anymore."

The wife came along, and I asked her. "Were you different before you were married?"

"Oh, yes, I was much more fun before he shaped me up. I'm not sure who I am now," she replied.

The man suddenly saw what he had done to her. He had taken a woman whose opposite traits he had fallen in love with and remade her to be like himself. When he got done, he wasn't happy with the results and neither was she. "What can I do now?" he asked me in a rare moment of vulnerability.

"You can take your hands off her, stop manipulating her life, and let some of her bright, engaging nature return."

"Would you? Would you?" she cried out to him.

He grabbed her, hugged her, and said, "I'm so sorry. I didn't know what I was doing."

Here was an exceptional Choleric-Melancholy who, when he saw his mistakes, was willing to apologize and change.

How Did People like Joyce Judging and Gilda Guilt Get This Way?

First, their inborn personality traits set the stage for their future. With their abilities, they overwhelmed their mothers, impressed their teachers, and manipulated their friends. They did it with such panache and at such an early age that others didn't see the possible danger in these strengths. Since they got away with it as children, they continued what had become winning skills for them and what had turned them into master manipulators of both family and friends.

Joyce tells people what's wrong with them and assumes they are grateful to hear so they can improve. She once said to me "I should think everyone would want to do things better." Few want to hear it from Joyce.

Gilda controls by guilt: "If you loved me, you would..." "If you respected my opinion, you would..." "You've never really cared..." She loves to shame people into helping her.

What Do They Want in Life?

Since they are both controlling Cholerics and creative Melancholies in one person, their inner desire is to remake people and situations to their perfect specifications. They don't see anything negative in this, as obviously anyone would be happier surrounded by those who are agreeable clones of themselves. Haven't you seen leaders who were followed by little imitations of themselves who looked, walked, sat, and gestured in similar styles? Sometimes whole churches take on the color of the pastor.

Recently I spent a week with a lady whose husband had been remaking her for years. He had been so successful that her words were his words. Whatever the group discussed, she would add, "Well, Dick says..." After a few days we asked, "Don't you have an opinion of your own? We don't want to hear what Dick thinks—we want to know what *you* think." She couldn't think of anything to say. She hadn't had a truly independent thought in years.

The Choleric-Melancholy only wants to correct wrongs and bring others up to his high standards. The goals are commendable, but the success turns out people who don't really know who they are and are seeking help from pastors and counselors who aren't sure how they got this way either.

Choleric-Melancholy women try to remake their husbands and are very influential in producing children in their image, no matter what the child's own personality may be. They always like the child best who shows enthusiasm for their constant direction, and they spend less time with the one who shows no desire to be a "before-and-after" example. They mold one and consider the other to be rebellious.

How Can We Get Along with Joyce Judging?

Listen and learn. If we're not married to this person, we can listen politely to her suggestions of character improvement and say, "I'll surely give that some thought." Then do give it some thought. Often her ideas are excellent and if put into effect will bring about positive results. What if her ideas don't fit you at all? Then don't put them on. Thank her for her time and interest.

If you are married to the person, you have a more serious problem because the Choleric-Melancholy wants to be in charge and will unconsciously remake you. We've had good results with using the Personality Profile as a springboard to meaningful conversation. If you can make taking this profile seem like an affirmation of the person's strengths, he or she is usually smart enough, with your help, to identify at least a few little inconsequential weaknesses.

If you point out how much happier you'd both be if you could return to your natural personality, your mate should at least give this some thought. Since the Choleric-Melancholy wants things to be right, a possible improvement might be appealing. Ask how he or she feels about you and your basic personality, and then listen. Even if you don't agree, you'll make the Choleric-Melancholy happy with your attention.

Ask what's new. Since the Choleric-Melancholy takes every course he isn't teaching, he always knows the latest trends and will love you if you'll ask what's new, and then listen. If you choose to offer a conflicting opinion, it's always safer if you quote from *Time* or Tom Brokaw than from your very own mind.

What Do I Care What Joyce Judging or Anyone Else Thinks of Me?

Many of us get far too upset with what other people think. Why? Because our own self-image is so shaky that we find it difficult to handle critical words from other people.

People like Joyce love to drop judgment on those who will react. If they find you are secure enough not to fall apart when taunted, they'll leave you alone and go on to those they can upset. It's no fun judging others if it doesn't bother them. I've watched a whole string of Judgings parade through various women's groups and try to scuttle the president. Those who could smile, say "Thank you," and move on were soon left alone, while those who got easily shaken were picked on.

Ask yourself whether it really matters what other people think. Our aim is to please the Lord and not worry about those people whose hobby it is to stir up trouble in the ranks.

What About Joyce's Eyes for the Minister of Music?

Joyce sets down the rules for others but bends them for herself. What can you do when you sense there is some romantic sideplay in the church? We all hope these worldly thoughts won't invade our group, but often they do. I've found that frequently the music department has its own secret soap opera circling the organ pipes. Why? Because musical people are unusually creative and artistic and have deep emotions. There's something about singing in harmony that makes people think they could live in harmony—if only they could get rid of that off-key mate who's always marching to the beat of a different drummer.

They start out with good motives: They love to sing. Then some get into the wrong choir robe when they only meant to get into the choir. One pastor's wife came crying to me that her husband was having an affair with the soprano. He was, and they were practicing duets late at night alone in church.

The wife of the evangelism pastor at one church pointed out that her husband seemed devoted to the organist. At lunch I saw her waving to me, and as I looked up she was standing behind her husband's chair pointing down to his arm that was around the other woman, right there in broad daylight, in church, on Sunday noon!

Recently one of our CLASS staff sat at a table with two couples and heard an ex-pastor and his new wife conversing with a professional gospel singer and her new husband. He asked, "Did you know your ex-husband was having an affair with my ex-wife while we were all still married?"

What's Happened?

We're just catching up with the world and looking at the choir loft as the Lido Deck on *The Love Boat*. We're looking out for number one, doing our own thing, and finding a friend in our field of vibrations. The *Dallas Morning News* had a full-page article on a new idea: We can have good close friends of the opposite sex without romantic involvement. It's possible but not likely.

What Should We Do?

The church has to forget its middle-of-the-road, look-the-other-way attitude and start teaching God's laws on sex and marriage. The evangelical churches have pretended there is no problem. One pastor told me, "We try to look the other way because we don't want to embarrass anyone."

Years ago our CLASS was in the Bethel Church in San Jose, California, and we went to the Sunday evening service. Pastor Charles Crabtree dared take a stand. He gave a bold and potent message with a three-point outline:

> Sexual Dominance
> Sexual Deviation
> Sexual Damnation

He let his people know that he would no longer tolerate sexual sin in the body of Christ. He based his directions on Paul's writings to the church at Corinth.[11] There was no one in that large congregation that night who did not get the point.

Surely we don't want a witch-hunt in the church, but neither can we condone incest and adultery. One of our authors, Jan Frank, who wrote *Door of Hope,* spoke on a Christian talk show on incest and got so many calls on the subject that she couldn't begin to answer them. Those victims who called in said they didn't know anyone in the Christian community cared about them. Many had talked to pastors who had told them either that it was their imagination, that they were trying to stir up trouble, or that they should forget the whole incident and forgive the offender.

Jan has offered her services to local churches to counsel girls with incest problems and has been told by some, "We don't have that problem in our church." She has started support groups for victims and is an abuse counselor and popular speaker.

Dr. Ted Cole once gave a very clear sermon directed toward the young men of his church: "You can lead a girl to bed, but can you lead her to the Lord?" That's surely a provocative question.

While we shouldn't look for trouble, we should have a procedure for dealing with the difficult person who gets himself into a compromising position. In Matthew 18:15-17, the Lord Jesus gives four steps in redeeming, not condemning, the person at fault.

1. Go to him privately and hope to win him back.

2. If he won't listen, take one or two other people with you as witnesses.

3. If he still won't listen, take the matter before the church (presumably the board of elders or deacons).

4. If he won't listen to the church and repent, remove him from the fellowship.

Before you go to straighten out the other person, remember that the Lord also said, "Let him without sin cast the first stone."[12]

What Should We Do with Gilda Guilt?

Life is full of people like Gilda who manipulate others and enjoy seeing how many they can "do in." It's a hobby akin to the old Indian chiefs who hung scalps off their belts to show the size of their collections. Mothers of young children are always fair game for Gildas, who make comments like:

"We never had sitters in our day."

"We really cared for our children."

"Johnny's mother got him a bike just like that and didn't watch him either. He was killed in traffic the very next day."

Some of you may have had a Gilda mother making statements like:

"The only reason I'm staying with your father and enduring this agony is for you."

"We could be in a big house today if we hadn't put you through college."

"For all the wedding cost, you could have at least stayed married to the bum."

Write a book. If you have a genuine Gilda Guilt who is frequently in your way, why not put together a humorous book on her sayings? Gildas have a golden talent, and it would be a shame to let it fade out of this generation without recording the guilt gems.

Even if you don't intend to write a real book, your attitude about Gilda will change when you appreciate what a reservoir of colorful material she can provide.

Say no. If you'd rather fight than write, refuse to go along with Gilda's comments:

"Don't you have time to look at the new baby clothes from the shower?" Reply: "I'm sure they're lovely, but I have no time tonight."

"I told them you'd come to the New Year's Eve party." Answer: "You didn't ask me first, and I'm not able to go."

"We bought this big turkey just for you." Respond: "That was so thoughtful, but we have other plans. Why don't you invite a new couple at church to come for dinner?"

A few pleasant but firm refusals will send Gilda looking for new game.

Don't let her drive. One of the great bastions of control for Gilda is the driver's seat. She promises you that this little run to the store for the spring sale will only take an hour. You agree to go even though you're tight on time. On the way to the store, she has to "just swing by the cleaners." As you sit in the car and wait, she seems to be praying over each plastic bag as it passes slowly by on the conveyor belt.

She and the cleaner girl seem to have developed a new friendship as they talk and laugh heartily together. When they finally embrace farewell, you realize you have just wasted 20 minutes.

Gilda goes to put the cleaning in the trunk, only to find it full of her husband's golf clubs and shoes.

She asks you if you'll come out and hold the cleaning while she rearranges the trunk. Here you are standing in a parking lot, holding long plastic bags high over your head and wondering how you ever got yourself in this position!

When you get to the sale, there's no place to park, and Gilda drives round and round looking for a spot.

You have no feel for even fantastic bargains at this point, and you suggest forgetting the whole idea and going home.

"Go home without even going to the sale!" gasps Gilda. "I should say not!"

You have no choice, so you enter, only to have Gilda lose herself in the bathrobes. You can't find her, and it's now time for you to be home getting dinner for your husband and his client. You finally find her in greeting cards, where she has determined to buy enough for every relative for the year. "Do you think this card would be good for Aunt Agnes, this one with the little rose-buds?"

"I don't even know Aunt Agnes."

"Well, aren't we a little huffy today!"

You beg her to leave her card selection for another day, and she mutters, "I could have saved at least ten dollars on these half-price cards if you weren't in such a hurry." You drive along in silence, but you no longer care because you're headed home— or are you?

"Why are we stopping at the funeral home?"

"Well, little old Mrs. Elkins died, and I knew you'd want to see the body." You are ready to strangle Gilda and toss her in with Mrs. Elkins.

If you know a Gilda Guilt, you've been on a few errands with her and lived to regret it. In the long run it'll be cheaper to take a taxi.

Martha Martyr

People tend to avoid Martha Martyr because they are sick of her stories of sorrow, sadness, and self-sacrifice. She's laden down with the weight of the world, and yet when someone volunteers to help, she turns them away with "I'll just do it all myself."

Martha is a strange mix: Melancholy, mournful, maligned, meek, and miserable—and yet with a Sanguine flair for the dramatic. When she tells you how put-upon she is, she stands tall, gestures grandly, and puts her hand upon her brow. Her sighs are audible across the room, and she saves her best stories for a spontaneously assembled audience. She always ends with a note that demands affirmation from the group.

> "Poor Martha—you really are dedicated to the church!"

> "Yes, you do the work of ten women. What would we ever do without you?"

Martha's moods swing wide from the Melancholy depths of depression to the Sanguine need for center-stage credit. Martha's children often ask, "What kind of mood is Mother in today?"

How Did Martha Get This Way?

Since the Melancholy-Sanguine combination in one person is an unnatural blend, that individual's insides are in a constant war. Their personality is split between Sanguine self-centeredness and Melancholy self-sacrifice. They want to give their all, and yet they need credit for doing it. This combination leads to "a double-minded man, unstable in all his ways." "Like a wave of the sea driven with the wind and tossed."[13]

How Does This Happen?

In our CLASS counseling, we have found that many of the Melancholy-Sanguines were initially Sanguines who went through some very difficult childhood experiences. Their natural exuberance for life was pressed down. They learned that, much as they wanted to enjoy each day, experience proved this to be a hopeless dream. The bubbles in the sunlight were pricked one by one, and the optimistic nature gave up and withdrew. Adversity did not put the bright lights out completely, but now they only flicker upon special occasions. When this person realizes their birth personality and prays to be restored, it is amazing how quickly the Lord transforms them.

Francine first tested as a Sanguine-Melancholy, but upon thoughtful, prayerful introspection, she realized that she was Sanguine in secure situations and Melancholy when she was insecure. One day when I was doing a Personality Plus seminar, I had Francine share her feelings. When she went out into the foyer, a flock of ladies followed her with similar personality splits and personal pains of the past.

Francine spent much time in prayer for wisdom and found that much of her Melancholy insecurity came from her emotional deprivation as the product of a split home and from some childhood traumas she had never faced.

Usually the Sanguine-Melancholy combination is a Sanguine who has an unexplainable depression coming from childhood trauma, but in Martha's case she is a Melancholy who had some of the Sanguine needs for love and attention brought on by her dismal childhood. Because of her father's apparent rejection of her and the family, plus her mother's desperate absorption with the daily duties necessary to hold life together, Martha Martyr learned from bitter experience. As Erma Bombeck wrote, "If life's a bowl of cherries, what am I doing here in the pits?"

Constant care and cleaning was Martha's mother's pattern to gain approval and compliments, and people in the church praise Martha in the same way for her dedication and self-denial. Without even a desire to follow in her mother's footsteps, Martha fell into a similar routine. How easy it is to reproduce our own weaknesses in our children without either side realizing what is happening!

Martha Martyr seems to be working her way to heaven, and because she never got credit or praise as a child, she is desperately seeking it today. Her mother brought her up in a legalistic church, and she still feels that plain clothes, no makeup, and abstention from anything fun are all signs of spirituality. She is her mother all over again.

What Does Martha Martyr Need in Life?

Martha Martyr has such a poor self-image, caused by financial and emotional deprivation as a child, that she could be given a big house and loving children but would still feel poor and rejected. On the surface she needs praise for her selfless work, but underneath she needs to be shown why she has this compulsion and a desire to be lifted up by others. She needs to see that the Christian life is not negative but abundant and that self-sacrifice can be carried to extremes.

How Do We Deal with Martha Martyr?

Because so many of Martha's problems stem from her past, it is difficult for us to deal with her on a superficial level; however, since few of us have the time to delve deeply, what can we do?

Give praise. Remember the principle *Find a need and fill it.* Martha's need is to have her poor self-image lifted. Her method of seeking is through good works. Other people with similar needs try to win through sports, social work, religious vocations, and platform ministries. Praise is the Band-Aid over the problems of the past, but unfortunately you can place patches of platitudes all over this person and he or she still would not be whole.

Examine the past. In our 30 years of ministry, we have learned that a high percentage of rape, incest, and other trauma victims go into social services or Christian work. Somehow the devastation of self-worth left from these experiences causes the victims to dedicate themselves to self-sacrificing ministries and helping professions. Although this is a generalization, we have found in our CLASS that more than one-fourth of each audience of Christian leaders has had a serious trauma in the past that is influencing their present behavior and inner needs.

While we cannot set ourselves up as amateur therapists, we can make ourselves available to listen to the inner thoughts of other people while being intelligently attuned to their possible problems of the past. It never ceases to amaze me how quickly a person with deep hurts will pour them out to a perfect stranger who has an accepting ear.

What should you do if someone does open up and disclose some past hurts? Sometimes seeing the connection between the past and the present will be healing in itself.

1. Let the person talk it out, as a compassionate listener can be a physician to the soul.

2. Refer the individual to a Christian counselor who deals with past pain and won't just tell the person to forget it.

3. Help him or her find a person trained in emotional inner healing using Christian principles.

4. Call our office for our book *Freeing Your Mind from Memories That Bind.* This book has changed more lives than all of our others put together. (1-800-433-6633)

Improve her looks. Although looks are only superficial, they can make a big difference in a woman's self-image. With the availability of health spas, success seminars, makeovers, color consultants, beauty shops, and other areas for self-improvement, we can always find a way to guide a person to the right spot. Never aim for drastic changes overnight, but gently encourage the person to positive change. So often Marita has found in consulting with women on color and fashion that, as they improve a little, people notice it and compliment them. Then they go a little further and sometimes surpass what she had dared to hope for.

We have found that self-confidence in dress and makeup can be a catalyst for positive change.

Joe Jock

Joe Jock is a pleasant person who would rather play games than get down to business. He is Sanguine (fun-loving and immature) and also Phlegmatic (easygoing and unmotivated). This combination emphasizes the light side of each personality, and Joe is truly all "fun and games."

Like Peter Pan, Joe has not yet grown up. His ex-wife got sick of babysitting him along with the children. He is a hero to those who participate with him in sports and a "hunk" to those who admire his laconic good looks, but when you have to count on Joe for support, his athletic prowess dims and his looks don't amount to much.

How Did Joe Get This Way?

Joe had a father who was addicted to sports and pushed him into ball games, and a doting mother who thought he was the cutest thing that ever chinned himself out of the crib. So often in sports-minded families, the game itself becomes more important than mental or emotional growth. The child becomes a family hero and subconsciously never wants to grow up and lose his status. Ribbons, cups, and statues adorn his room, and visitors are shown the results and rewards of his abilities. He lives in Never-Never Land and doesn't know that there's a real world out there. Some young men and women become pros, but the majority, like Joe, love to play but can't make a living on sports. Some come to this realization early enough to plan for the future, but many just keep playing games and hope to marry someone who will cheerfully support them.

When Fred and I were first married, we lived in an apartment next to a Joe Jock. He was a handsome man who drove a Cadillac and went out each morning with a tennis racket or golf clubs. One day his wife confessed to me that she had no money and no food—that she had not had a new dress in ages and she was trying not to let her mother know her situation. She explained how he would always find people to take him out to dinner. Because of his skill and his personality, others would pay him to play, and this gave him spending money for clothes. Because of his charm, he could postpone payments on his car and con people into supporting him. Joe seemed to float above the problems of life.

Here was a Cadillac body being driven around by a little boy. He was out at the ballpark while his family ate peanuts at home.

How Do You Get Along with Joe Jock?

It's easy to get along with Joe if you're on his team, but if you see beyond the muscles and suggest that he grow up, you become a member of the opposing side. If you live with him or work closely with him, you will soon grow weary of his immaturity, and you will become defeated when you realize that he has convinced his mother, father, friends, fans, and family that you are a dismal drag and don't appreciate him. Suddenly the boss or mate becomes the giant trying to cut down Joe's beanstalk, and he needs to go home to mother, who will agree with him that all these other people are wrong.

As with the alcoholic or any compulsive personality, as long as the cast keeps supporting and covering up his habit, he sees no reason to change. He has to hurt badly enough to want help. The best explanation of the part the supporting cast plays in helping the offender continue is a booklet put out by Al-Anon, "The Merry-Go-Round Called Denial."

If you are trying to deal with an addictive personality, whether it's sports, gambling, eating, drinking, lying, or drugs, get this booklet and attend an Al-Anon meeting to learn how to confront your problem person in a positive way.

Isn't Becoming a Christian Enough?

I have seen people who have prayed to receive Christ and been transformed overnight, but I have seen more who are made aware of their shortcomings and begin to work prayerfully and humanly to overcome them. If we all shaped up instantly, we would have heaven on earth, but we only need to look around our church or even our own family to find Christians who are still a little difficult to get along with.

Paul himself told of the struggle he had with his old nature and his new spiritual nature warring within him: "I do what I shouldn't do and don't do what I should do."[14]

And Jesus said, "With God all things are possible."[15] Not guaranteed or even probable, but possible.

So many women I counsel spend their whole marriages in purgatory waiting to be released into heaven on the day their husband receives the Lord. How much precious time we waste waiting for the Lord to reach down and shape up those difficult people!

We can hope that Joe Jock is at a turning point in his life. We can hope that the pastor will force him into a place of confronting himself realistically. He needs to see that if he wants to be an example to his children, he must grow up and become responsible. He must see the error of his ways and be willing to repent and ask forgiveness. When he is faced with a situation he can't charm his way out of, he should be listening to God's plan of salvation for his life. If he allows the Lord to deal deeply with his inner attitudes and if he is willing to change, Joe can become a living testimony to the power of God to transform lives. Otherwise he will spend his life seeking someone who will love him and support him and expect nothing in return.

Winnie Witness

Winnie Witness is an example of a good thing carried to extremes. Winnie has the best combination of temperaments for dynamic leadership because she is both Sanguine (outgoing, engaging, and conversant) and Choleric (assertive, tireless, and eager). These traits make a positive Christian leader, but, as with all attributes when they are pushed too far, this person becomes a compulsive talker who is overly aggressive.

How Did Winnie Get like This?

You may know a Winnie whose strength is overworked in a direction other than witnessing: This type of person latches on to causes and goes for it! Since her aims are usually positive, even altruistic, she can't imagine that anyone could be offended by her single-minded zeal coupled with endless enthusiasm. When the goal can also be looked upon as in God's will or a directive from some heavenly hotline, the perpetrator is even more eager to press on. We all know the thinking: The end justifies the means.

How Do Good Motives Get Carried to Extremes?

Since Winnie sees herself as a wonderful, witnessing believer, she feels compelled to get her husband into the kingdom. She has manipulated him into revivals, and he has been prayed for and shared with in every possible manner and situation. The more she pushes, the more he resists. He has allowed her to invite over her "religious friends" only if she promises not to have any "prayers or speeches." She promises, but she let us all know how ungodly he is by whispering the circumstances to us as we enter.

Fred and I attended such a party. We were given the clue, and some of us felt sorry for him.

The guests were all gracious and loving to the husband, and we were as shocked as he was when the lights went out suddenly and slides appeared on the wall of starving children in Africa. A young man arose from nowhere and gave a heart-rending plea for Christian commitment coupled with a collection for the children. As guests were nervously reaching for their wallets, the husband stormed out.

Our Winnie realized she had gotten too religious, so she shifted the subject from Africa by leading us all in a limp rendition of "There's a Shanty in Old Shanty-Town."

Many other times I have been in a situation where a Winnie has called upon me at a dinner party to share my testimony in hope of converting her husband, and even more times I've been told that I was invited to a party expressly to evangelize old Arthur Atheist. An eager Winnie gives me my assignment, leads me over to Arthur, gives him an introduction of me which makes me sound like an archangel, and pushes me onto the couch next to him. I can tell from his expression that I am one more in an ever-shifting line of junior Holy Spirits assigned to hover over his head. I also can sense that if I don't convert him, I will not have earned my supper.

When I spoke for my chaplain brother at an Air Force base, an officer took me out to lunch and presented me with a depressed teenager of questionable morals. He kept forcing me to counsel her, and I never did eat very much. When my brother mentioned his displeasure to the man, he replied, "Your sister's been in this game long enough to know that there's no such thing as a free lunch." The Winnies or Waldos of the world manipulate us all to do their work.

What Can We Do with Winnie?

As with so many difficult people, being forewarned is being forearmed. When we see a certain pattern of behavior, we have to decide ahead of time how we will handle it the next time.

We can't let Bob Bossy push us around.

We can't let Debbie Depressed pull us down.

Neither can we let zealots put us into difficult situations. If I'm at all suspicious, I now ask ahead, "What do you expect of me tonight?" If they act unsure of how to answer me, I ask again. "Did you want me to share, give my testimony, or lead your husband to the Lord?" (You could ask whatever you suspect the person is after: Entertain her old aunt, help with the dishes, babysit her children, etc. Get to the point.)

Once the person has vowed she has absolutely none of these things in mind, she can hardly ask you to perform—although the extreme case will try to trick you later, so be wary.

To get along positively with these positive people who carry positive thinking to extremes, we should realize that it is their single-mindedness of purpose that has made them successful in life. Most great historical heroes have been looked upon as fanatics by their cohorts. Their obsessive desire to achieve certain goals is why they often rise above the average.

Realizing this will help us to understand an overeager person, and if we find ourselves in a position to share helpfully, with a Winnie, we can applaud her aims but show her not to force everyone else to march to the beat of her internal drummer.

The world, the church, the office, and even the family may be dotted with difficult people.

Do you care enough to make an effort to get along with them?

Are you willing to find out what they need and give it to them?

Can you maintain a relationship even if they don't respond?

Can you confront in love when necessary?

Is your own self-image healthy enough that you don't need to worry about what other people think of you?

The following words from a little pamphlet, "This Thing Is from Me," put these questions in perspective:

> Are you in difficult circumstances, surrounded by people who do not understand you, who never consult your taste, who put you in the background? This thing is from Me. I am the God of circumstances. Thou camest not to thy place by accident; it is the very place God meant for thee. Have you not asked to be made humble? See, then, I have placed you in the very school where this lesson is taught; your surrounding and companions are only working out my will.[16]

Chapter 4

How Do the Difficult People See Us?

More than 40 years ago I was hired to teach a class entitled "Elementary Psychology," sponsored by the Adult Education Department of the New Haven, Connecticut, school system. When I asked for the text, the superintendent told me there was none. The teacher before me had developed notes over the years, but he had taken them all with him when he left. I had to write my own material.

With only two weeks before the start of school, I didn't have much time to delve deeply into the great psychologists. I made a list of 30 possible topics, duplicated the list, and passed it out the first night. The class was to rank the topics in the order of their interest, and I would custom-tailor the course to their needs. They were excited that I cared enough to design the course just for them, and they worked away at the list. I had offered topics ranging from overcoming shyness to Freud's theory of dream interpretation. Since I had no knowledge of Freud's theory, I was relieved when he landed in last place, just below schizophrenia. The most popular of all the choices was "getting along with other people."

The next week I asked the class to list all the things they didn't like about these "other people," and then I tabulated their choices. At the top of the list were:

Complainers
Conceited people

85

Braggers
Hypocritical people
Loud attention-getters
Gossipers
People who don't like what I say
Those who give criticism and can't take it
Liars
Those who steal and cheat
Bullies
Tattletales
Bigots

and on and on, ending with

Aspiring Doris Days

What a list of difficult people! If we handled only one kind a night, it would take the whole course just to get through them.

I wondered: If there were so many difficult people in New Haven, were any of them in my class? The next week I asked them to list their own faults and found that none of the bad people they all knew were in the room! Instead, I had a group with insignificant little weaknesses:

Inferiority complex
Overeating
Withdrawn
Bad voice
Not natural enough
Poor willpower
Procrastinator
Lazy
Preoccupied
Giggle a lot
Daydreamer
Can't stand some people, but hide it so they won't know.

Isn't it amazing that other people have serious faults like bragging and complaining while we giggle and daydream? I kept the list. Since then I have done this same exercise with different groups, but always with similar results: Those other people are really difficult, but I'm not so bad myself.

Over the years we haven't changed all that much; we've just become more wrapped up in ourselves. During the '70s we went through what was called the *me* generation. We were told that it was time to think of ourselves, examine our psyche, and do our own thing. We were to throw old-fashioned morals and principles aside (because they had been holding us down) and instead develop to our full potential.

Seminars were offered to lead us to ultimate fulfillment, and people paid to be emptied of the ethics that had held them down. As the world went rushing into ego-centered activities, we were told that this new freedom would bring happiness to us all. But has it? A cover article in *Time* magazine says, "What women who tried to break out of traditional relationships found is that it doesn't work."[17]

We've spent years learning to look out for number one, but all we've come up with is people who no longer make an effort to get along with anyone else. It's always the other person's fault. "If you don't like the way I function, then get out." So people have gotten out. The family is no longer a group trying for some kind of unity and harmony, but separate individuals who for a time are living under the same roof. Everyone is working for the luxuries that we now see as necessities, and the children are being brought up in day care centers. "Latchkey kids" is an expression used for the thousands of children who come home to an empty house and are free to "do their own thing" until dinnertime.

Even though we as Christians feel we are not part of the world, we acquire the mode of society without realizing what we're doing. I wish we were apart from these problems, but we're not. At one CLASS we had 100 above-average Christian leaders in attendance. Although our goal is to train leaders, not solve emotional problems, we have learned that it's hard to be an effective Christian leader when you are not sure who you are or what to do about the conflicts in your own life.

We teach the personalities and suggest that each individual evaluate himself. Many of these people haven't ever examined their strengths and weaknesses and some have pain from the past that is preventing their functioning well in the present. One lady wrote me, "While at CLASS my group leader helped me to see that my husband wasn't my problem. I had blamed every-thing on him and I was ruining our marriage. I found out I was taking out on him the hostility I felt toward my father. Just under-standing what I was doing to my husband has made a tremen-dous difference. Both of us feel as if a weight were lifted from us, and now I'm beginning to deal with the right problem instead of looking at my husband as an impossible person."

When I do parts of this book as a skit, I always ask the audi-ence how many of them have seen a character who reminds them a little of themselves. Every hand goes up.

We all have some minor weakness that could use improve-ment. As Robert Burns, the Scottish poet, wrote in 1776,

> "Oh wad some power the giftie gie us, to see oursels as others see us."[18]

We as Christians do have problems. We all have difficult people to deal with, and sometimes the difficult person is our-selves.

Just as important as seeing how we can get along with others is asking, "How do others see us? Do we show some of the same traits as the cast of the *Parade of Pious Personalities?* Are we sometimes critical of others, like Joyce Judging? Do we take pride in our scriptural knowledge, like Sally Spiritual? Are we forcing a quick commitment on every unsuspecting person, like Winnie Witness? Are we tearing around doing good works, like Harriet Hurry? Are we complaining about how much we do for others and how little credit we get, like Martha Martyr? Do we have a record of wrongs in our head about those who have hurt us and don't deserve to be forgiven, like Gertrude Grudge? Are we constantly downcast and knocking ourselves in hope that others will boost our ego, like Debbie Depressed?

The Bible tells us in Colossians 3 to "put to death" our old selves, to take off the old clothes and put on the new. What old clothes do you have to take off? Each year when we women buy new clothes, we don't put them on over the old. We don't put a light, fluffy dress over a long-sleeved wool sweater. We first take off the old and then put on the new. In our Christian lives we often ignore this principle and try to jam a new life on top of our old habits. In Colossians, Paul tells us that we are the people of God, that He loved us and chose us for His own. Therefore, because we are His, we must take off the old habits and put on the new clothes.

Do you need some new clothes? Could you use some kindness, some genuine humility, some flowing gentleness, some appealing patience? Would you choose a helpful spirit that doesn't have to be trimmed with credit? Would you look better wearing a wide belt of love that would bind you together in perfect unity? Or do you need a pocket of peace placed over your heart?

What are your needs today? A skirt of kindness, a patch of patience, a belt of love, a pocket of peace? Or do you need the whole new wardrobe?

Let's listen in on a rehearsal for the future segments of the *Parade of Pious Personalities* and hear what instructions the director has to give the cast. If you've found some little part of yourself in Debbie Depressed or Bob Bossy, you might apply these suggestions to yourself, knowing that the Lord wants you to take off your old clothes and put on the new.

Let's call back our cast of the *Parade of Pious Personalities*. Marvin, bring your musicians out front. Come on down, Sally Spiritual, Debbie Depressed and G-Clef Girls, and let's get Joyce Judging at the organ.

Sam, come to the platform where you belong, and bring Bob Bossy with you. Harriet, hurry in from the nursery. Larry Lazy, Winnie Witness and Joe Jock, come down from the back row, and would someone wake up Martha Martyr, who's so exhausted from her hard work? As these characters come forth, all committed believers who are still wearing their old carnal clothes, let's take another look at them. These are the leaders of the new Big Brown Church on the Move. Do they look familiar? Have you ever been in a church led by people like this? Have you ever been one of them yourself?

Sally Spiritual, you're always first. God is so pleased with your desire for spiritual food, and the Christian bookstore considers you its best customer. The church is grateful for your timeless service, and the community applauds your high morals. However, no one really likes to be with you. Your friends are tired of your sermons and your family is fatigued by your verses. Living with you is like taking a lifelong lecture course with no hope of graduation. Sally, you have been answering questions that no one has even asked.

Your children feel that they are in competition with God for your attention. You have shown too much church and not enough Christ. Sally, are you willing to come down from your spiritual steeple and relax with the rest of us? The Bible says, "Pride goeth before...a fall."[19] Paul says, "Let him that thinketh he standeth take heed lest he fall."[20] Sally, it's time for you to give some loving attention to your family before you lose them. Take heed, Sally, lest you fall.

In Matthew 5:16 Jesus Himself explains what your attitude should be: "Let your light, Sally, so shine before men that they may see your good works and glorify your Father who is in heaven." Your aim of Christian service is to glorify God, not to give credit unto Sally.

Are you willing to take off your old clothes all pleated with pride and put on your new apron of humility?

Marvin Music, leave your worries on the altar and come forth. God appointed you to come before His presence with singing. He does not want you to labor over each note and wear down the choir with endless rehearsals. He is more excited about a positive attitude than a perfect pitch. "Make a joyful noise unto God, all ye lands: Sing forth the honor of his name; make his praise glorious....All the earth shall worship thee, and shall sing unto thee."[21]

Yes, Marvin, it is right that you make a joyful noise, that you lead your people in psalms of praise, that you sing for the honor of His name.

How easy it is to push for perfection and lose sight of the goal! God has not called you to coach a choir of heavenly angels, but to inspire the members to sing praises to the Lord and let them enjoy doing it.

Marvin, take off your old choir robe of perfection and put on the new one of joy.

Sam Sermon, God has appointed and ordained you that you go and bring forth fruit,[22] that you should preach peace by Jesus Christ.[23] God has promised His people that He will give them pastors according to His heart who will feed the flock with knowledge and understanding.[24]

Sam, you have such a gift for delivery and such a sense of humor, but you are more interested in having fun than feeding the flock. Remember Solomon's wise words: "When a good man speaks, he is worth listening to, but the words of fools are a dime a dozen."[25] You don't spend enough time in searching the Scriptures, and your sermons are shallow and lacking in substance. You are the shepherd, and you are to feed the church of God. "Woe to the shepherds who feed themselves instead of their flocks."[26]

Sam, you have such potential, but you've not disciplined your life. You're hoping to stumble over the finish line when you haven't set a serious goal. Paul tells us to do all things "decently and in order,"[27] and this should be your new aim in life. Study to show yourself approved unto God, organize your time even if it hurts, pull yourself together, and grow up. Stop making yourself the center of the church, and instead preach the glory of the Lord Jesus.

Sam, are you ready to remove the rompers of potential and put on the business suit of order?

Joyce Judging, would you come forward? Joyce, God is pleased because you have studied the Scriptures and have learned the rules of Christian living; however, He is not happy with your judgmental attitude. You grieve the Lord when you criticize other people in His name. God is a God of loving kindness, and He does not want you measuring the faults of others with your big yardstick of life. Stop preaching at your children, correcting all your friends, weighing the mistakes of the minister, and siphoning up the sins of your husband. Learn to accept imperfect people just as they are, for that's how the Lord has accepted you.

Matthew 7:1 says, "Judge not, that ye be not judged." This is an admonition to you, Joyce, straight from the Lord. "Judge not, that ye be not judged: for with what judgment ye judge, ye shall be judged, and with what measure ye mete, it shall be measured to you again."[28] In Ephesians 4:29 there is a verse of priceless instruction. It says, "Let no corrupt communication proceed out of your mouth, but that which is good to the use of edifying, that it may minister grace unto the hearers."[29]

Joyce, corrupt communication is anything that hurts or hinders the growth of another person. Let no corrupt word proceed out of your mouth. Instead, Joyce, say only things that will edify or build up others—things that will encourage your children, minister grace to your growth group, do a favor for your friends, and give a verbal gift to your husband.

Joyce, stop staring wishfully at Marvin Music, as the Lord Himself said that if we look on another person with lust in our hearts, we have sinned already.[30] Hear the advice of your God and know that "winking at sin leads to sorrow; bold reproof leads to peace."[31]

Joyce, are you willing to take off the Mosaic robe of judgment and stop flirting with temptation? Are you willing to speak with kindness, not criticism? To minister grace, not give out advice?

Joyce, lay down your "thou shalt nots" and put on a new cloak of kindness.

Bob Bossy, the church sure needs your direction and wisdom. You have a brilliant business sense and the people respect you, but many resent your lofty airs, wonder why you park in a "No Parking" spot, and want to scream when your beeper goes off during the benediction. Are you really so much better than the rest of us that you can set your own rules? "Woe unto them that are wise in their own eyes, and prudent in their own sight!"[32]

No one likes a bossy person, a Pharisee who is above the rest, who takes the law into his own hands. Paul says that we should all be of the same mind and "love one another warmly as Christian brothers, and be eager to show respect for one another....Share your belongings with your needy fellow Christians, and open your homes to strangers....Do not think of yourself more highly than you should. Instead, be modest in your thinking....You must obey the authorities—not just because of God's punishment, but also as a matter of conscience."[33]

The church body appreciates your ability, and the pastor needs your business balance, but, as the Bible says, the people dislike those who "trust in their wealth and boast themselves in the multitude of their riches."[34]

Bob, are you willing to pop your buttons of boasting, bragging, and bossing, and instead bind yourself together with a belt of brotherly love?

Debbie Depressed, God is happy with your deeply sensitive nature. It's good that you are able to see problems and solve them; however, your whole life is one of discouragement and disappointment.

A black cloud is traveling with you, and it doesn't seem to have a silver lining. You wear your depression like an old bathrobe, and you're not willing to take it off and get dressed. You are wrapped up in yourself and your problems, and you don't see any way out.

You ask everyone for help, but you're not willing to take action on their advice. You take pills to wake you up and to calm you down, and sometimes even the pills get their purpose confused.

Debbie, would you really like to feel better? Would you really like to smile without hurting your face? Are you willing to trust God with your life and believe that He can do something with you? The Bible promises that when we ask Jesus into our heart, He *will* come in and give us peace.[35]

Debbie, you have Jesus in your heart, and He wants to lift your burdens. While your circumstances may not change, Jesus is able to give you that peace, which passes all human understanding.

Debbie, put down your pills and your puppy. Take off the old signs of depression and put on your new pocket of peace. Remember, "Thou wilt keep him in perfect peace whose mind is stayed on thee."[36]

Harriet Hurry, come on over! Harriet, the Lord is so impressed with how much you accomplish every day, and with how many different organizations you can run at the same time. You have your clocks set correctly and your calendars coordinated, but you have no time for family or friends. Your projects take precedence over people.

Are you afraid to sit down and face yourself? Is your frenzy a cover-up for insecurity? Do you keep busy so you won't know you're miserable inside? Are you always leaving for somewhere? Do your children only know you from the rear?

Harriet, maybe it's time for you to slow down, to put your priorities in order. Psalm 46:10 says, "Be still and know that I am God." How can God speak to you when your feet, hands, and mouth are always going? Harriet, relax, be still, and listen to

God's plan for your life. "You need to be patient, in order to do the will of God and receive what he promises."[37]

What does God have in mind for you, Harriet? Are you willing to forsake your frenzy and sit on the sideline for a season?

Harriet Hurry, take off your track shoes and cover the emblem on your sweatshirt with a patch of patience.

Martha Martyr, you are the martyr of us all. You sacrifice while we sit. You scrub while we smile. You sigh while we sing. It must seem unfair that you do all the work while we have all the fun.

God is pleased with your devotion to duty, your mothering the missionaries, and your avoidance of frivolity and fun. Yet, Martha, why are you so anxious to work and so eager for acclaim? Is it possible that you want to clean at the right hand of the Father in heaven? Do you want to have more gold stars on your celestial chart than the other saints?

Jesus visited a lady named Martha who was a lot like you. Martha was overoccupied, encumbered, and distracted with too much housework and cooking. She came up to the Lord and asked Him, "Is it nothing to you that my sister has left me to serve alone?" She wanted to make sure the Lord noticed how put-upon she was while her sister sat at the feet of Jesus doing nothing productive. Martha went on to say, "Tell her to help me, to lend a hand and to do her part along with me."

But the Lord replied, "Martha, Martha! You are worried and troubled over so many things."[38]

Martha, you *are* anxious and troubled about many things. While Mary learns from the Lord, you are working your way to heaven. You are fretting, fussing, and fuming, all for worldly credit. Martha, you don't have to wash all the dishes and weep. You don't have to collect used clothes and collapse. You could do what others really need done, and then not wait for the praises. Jesus says to you, "When you help a needy person, do it in such a way that even your closest friend will not know about it. Then it will be a private matter. And your Father, who sees what you do in private, will reward you."[39]

Martha, are you willing to lay aside your self-pity and spirit of martyrdom and be genuinely helpful to those in need, without telling your friends or giving a public testimony?

Martha, put down your old sacks of servitude and fill up your handbag with helpfulness.

Larry Lazy, you are light and lovable. You get along with everyone and keep peace at all costs, but the men on the board can't count on you and the women are tired of your wife requesting prayer to heal the hole in your roof. Larry, why don't you get up out of the chair and get moving? Change your motto about problems—"If you ignore them they'll go away." Don't keep saying, "It's easier to endure the problem than solve it."

When we gave you the "Passive Recipient Award," we didn't think that you'd wear it, and when you got the La-Z-Boy chair for your birthday, we didn't know you'd retire in it.

Larry, the Bible tells us, "A lazy fellow is a pain to his employers—like smoke in their eyes or vinegar that sets the teeth on edge."[40] You've set your wife's teeth on edge. It's time you stop thinking of your own relaxation, and instead assume your responsibility as a husband and a father.

"Work hard and become a leader; be lazy and never succeed."[41] Larry Lazy, the whole church wants you to succeed. "Be strong...and work, for I am with you, saith the Lord of hosts."[42]

Larry, are you willing to lay aside your lounge clothes and pick up the tools of the trade?

Winnie Witness, we need you! How every Christian group needs an eager witness! God is so excited with your willing spirit. He loves to hear you share your testimony and recite salvation verses. But, Winnie, you have offended people whom you meant to help because you came on too strong. Do you remember the woman who almost missed her plane because you wouldn't let her out of the ladies' room until you got to Law Four? Do you remember the little girl who went home crying because you'd gripped her too tightly with your Good News Gloves? Think of how withdrawn your husband has been since you told him he'd never get to heaven.

Winnie, God wants you to witness, but try to be sensitive to other people's feelings. Not every coffee hour has to be turned into a tent meeting. Not every luncheon must be an evangelistic rally. Winnie, don't lose your zeal, but couple it with a gentle spirit. Let people see Christ in you and know that your changed life is genuine.

Winnie, some good advice for you is found in 1 Peter 3:1,2,4 TEV: "You wives must submit yourselves to your husbands, so that if any of them do not believe God's word, your conduct will win them over to believe. It will not be necessary for you to say a word, for they will see how pure and reverent your conduct is....Your beauty should consist of your true inner self, the ageless beauty of a gentle and quiet spirit, which is of the greatest value in God's sight."

Winnie, go home and start to *love* your husband, not condemn him. Make him want to be like you, not work against you. Let him see God's Word in action in your life, for when he sees how pure and reverent your conduct is, he will believe God's truth and you will not have to say a word. Aim for that sweet and gentle spirit, which is of great value in the sight of both God and man. Also know that "the servant of the Lord must not strive, but be gentle unto all men."[43]

Winnie, are you willing to put your old plastic Good News Gloves in your pocket and put on the new gloves of gentleness?

Joe Jock, you are a winner in many ways, but you're a loser in marriage. You've put games before growth, and it's time for a change. Paul says, "When I was a child, I spake as a child, I understood as a child, I thought as a child; but when I became a man, I put away childish things."[44]

Joe, if you wish to function productively in an adult world, you must put away childish things. You must grow up to Christ, who is your head. As a new Christian you should picture yourself as a working part of the body of Christ. You've already trained your physical body, and now you must use yourself as a part of the spiritual body. "Under his control all the different parts of the body fit together, and the whole body is held together by every joint with which it is provided. So when each separate part works as it should, the whole body grows and builds itself up through love."[45]

Joe, God wants you to be a part of the body of Christ. There's nothing wrong with physical activities (Paul stressed keeping our bodies in shape), but the difference is in our priorities.

Go back to your wife and tell her you have a new life. Find out what she needs from you and give it to her; the Lord wants you to love your wife as you love your own body.[46]

Don't worry, Joe, about getting out of shape as you work on your spiritual body. "For this reason we never become discouraged. Even though our physical being is decaying, yet our spiritual being is renewed day after day."[47]

Joe, there is such excitement in store for you as you grow up in Christ. Are you ready to throw aside your concern with your outward nature and put on an inward nature that will be made new day after day?

Gilda Guilt, you are an active and dynamic individual, and you can accomplish more in a given time than the average woman. You write, speak, preside, and teach. God has observed your good works and the blessing you've been to others. As a Christian leader, you need to realize how controlling you are over the lives of other people. You're not satisfied to guide the girls—you order their steps in your chosen direction.

You are giving and hospitable, but you quietly demand submission of those whom you entertain. Learn to have a one-to-one relationship without taking charge: "One that hath friends must show himself friendly, and there is a friend that sticketh closer than a brother."[48]

A friend cares about the feelings of other people and doesn't need to have control. "Love is...never haughty or selfish or rude. Love does not demand its own way. It is not irritable or touchy. It does not hold grudges and will hardly even notice when others do it wrong."[49]

Gilda, do you want to have friends who will enjoy your company and seek you out? Then let them have their way. Let them make decisions, and cease manipulating the minds of other people. No one is ever at ease when he senses he is being used and has been put under a cloak of guilt.

Gilda, throw off that old cloak of guilt and wrap up your friends in love.

Gloria Gossip, come forward. You have an engaging personality, and you love to talk on the phone. Your stories are creative and entertaining, but you often exaggerate and elaborate, and the truth has never stood in the way of a tall tale. While your wit is winsome, a few women have been hurt when you passed on a confidence to others. Some prayer requests have taken on a whole new hue when passed through your colorful mind to your awaiting mouth. It's time for you to stop and think before you speak and ask yourself if what you're saying might offend the subject of the story. When you hear your mouth about to say:

• My opinion is...

• It's none of my business, but...

• The way I heard it was...

• I probably shouldn't say this, but...

Don't!

You may think you are amusing others, but the Bible calls your constant comments *gossip.*

"A gossip goes around spreading rumors, while a trustworthy man tries to quiet them."[50]

"An evil man sows strife; gossip separates the best of friends."[51]

"Their wives...must be of good character and must not gossip."[52]

Gloria, the Lord wants you to curb your tongue, and He says to you, "Don't talk so much. You keep putting your foot in your mouth. Be sensible and turn off the flow!"[53]

He wants you to use your head. "From a wise mind comes careful and persuasive speech. Kind words are like honey— enjoyable and healthful."[54]

Gloria, you have so much to offer your friends and the church body, but you must learn to control your tongue and not hurt others, for "a beautiful woman lacking discretion and modesty is like a fine gold ring in a pig's snout."[55]

Gloria, are you willing to change? Can you take off the bold and brassy words of gossip and put on the fine gold ring of truth?

Gertrude Grudge, come forth and bring your book. Gertrude, God is pleased that you have superior ability and that you display a discerning spirit. Gertrude, you must take off your unforgiving attitude and learn what God expects of you. As God forgives us, so He desires that we forgive others. He says, "I will forgive their iniquity, and I will remember their sin no more."[56] God forgives us and *forgets, not records,* our failures. He puts our sins as far as the East is from the West. He hides our sins in the depths of the ocean. He blots out our transgressions. But you, Gertrude, enjoy recording the failures of others so you can feel self-righteous. Listen to God's words written especially for you:

"If ye forgive men their trespasses, your heavenly Father will also forgive you."[57]

"When ye stand praying, forgive, if ye have aught against any: that your Father also which is in heaven may forgive you your trespasses."[58]

How often should you forgive someone? "If he trespass against thee seven times in a day...thou shalt forgive him."[59]

"Be ye kind one to another, tenderhearted, forgiving one another, even as God for Christ's sake hath forgiven you."[60]

Gertrude, stop keeping grudges and stop recording all the failures of other people. Lay down your *Record of Wrongs* and wrap yourself up in the scarf of forgiveness.

How about you? Have you asked the Lord into your life to give you peace? Have you taken off your old clothes and put on the new, or are you hanging some Christian accessories over the same old you? Are you wearing the cloak of kindness? Are you willing to don the apron of humility? Can you sew on at least a patch of patience? Can you carry the handbag of helpfulness? Will you wrap yourself and your friends in the scarf of forgiveness? Are you willing to tie your whole life together with the belt of love? And do you know where to find that pocket of perfect peace?

If you've seen areas in your life that need a change, be willing to take off your old clothes and to choose a whole new wardrobe for the rest of your life.

So our hope for you
As we gather today
Is to take off the old clothes
And throw them away.

To put on a fresh set
All sparkling and new
And know that God loves us,
He loves you and you.

He'll give you new clothes
They won't cost a dime
So thank you for coming
We'll see you next time.

Chapter 5

How Did Paul Handle
a Difficult Situation?

Before I started studying the Bible seriously, I had always thought of Paul as some super-saint. I saw him more as a marble statue than as a person, and I imagined that his many writings had been etched in stone. As I began to read of him, he slowly took form as a human being and very soon became my friend.

How does an apostle become a friend? How does anyone become a friend? First you spend time with him, then you find some mutual interest, and suddenly you really care about him. As Paul himself explained in Philippians 3:10 TEV, "All I want is to *know* Christ and to *experience* the power of his resurrection, to *share* in his sufferings and *become* like him...."

As I spent time in Paul's words, as I read of his trials and his problems, I could feel his power through the pages, and I soon saw that I was much like him. Paul and I are both Choleric, powerful personalities, born leaders, ready to take on the world in our own strength. The Lord Jesus humbled us both, gave us both situations over which we had no control, let us both have a touch of humor in heavy situations, and sent us both out to teach truth to "difficult" people.

The first book of the Bible I ever taught was Colossians, and I fell in love with the spirit of Paul. One day I found his letter to Philemon, and I saw how skillfully Paul handled a very difficult human relations problem.

Philemon was a wealthy silk merchant from Colosse who discovered his need for the Savior at a forum in Ephesus where he was selling his wares. Paul was the speaker, shared his testimony, remained to be available, and had personally led Philemon to the Lord.

Oh, Paul, how I relate to you! How many hundreds of times have I given my testimony, and how often have I stayed to share with a questioning lady of a heavy heart!

As Philemon grew in his faith, he opened his home to new Christians, and soon a church developed from their fellowship. Philemon evangelized his friends, his family, and some of his slaves, but one slave, Onesimus, felt his owner was a hypocrite. How could Philemon say there is no Greek or Jew, master or slave—all are one in Christ—and then not free his slaves? How could he preach the love of the Lord and expect Onesimus to believe him?

One day this bright and willful slave ran away. Who knows what he took of Philemon's possessions to provide transportation to Rome and freedom at last. Onesimus learned, however, as so many young people find once they have run away from home, that there's not always freedom in the free lifestyle.

Onesimus found himself friendless and without funds in Rome and remembered that Paul was imprisoned there. He recalled how Paul had spoken kindly to him in Ephesus and had not looked down upon him as a slave. Onesimus inquired until he found Paul in jail. Paul remembered him, welcomed him, counseled him, and led him to the Lord. As they prayed and shared together, Paul, who was constantly chained to a guard, explained to Onesimus that he had been wrong to run away and that now as a believing Christian he should return to Colosse, confess his sins to his master, and ask forgiveness.

Since the law allowed masters to kill runaway slaves, Onesimus was not enthused over his future prospects. Paul was faced with a difficult human relations problem. How could he convince his friend Philemon to accept and forgive this slave, especially when he couldn't visit him, talk face to face, or call him on the phone?

Paul on his own had never been noted for his charm, and had been heavy-handed in dealing with people who didn't see things his way. In fact, some people found him difficult. But God had worked miracles in Paul as he had become willing to submit his life to the Lord. He had said himself while in jail in Philippi, "God is always at work in you to make you *willing* and *able* to obey his own purpose."[61]

Paul had a problem, a purpose, and a plan. He would write to Philemon.

How would you handle this situation? Do you have a human relations problem in your life today? Do you need some helpful steps to restore peace to your path?

Let's look at Paul's approach to a difficult situation.

Compliments

Paul starts on a positive note:

> To our friend and fellow worker Philemon, and to the church that meets in your house...may God our Father and the Lord Jesus Christ give you grace and peace.[62]

Knowing that his letters were always read to the fellowship, Paul began his message with compliments. "Philemon, you are my friend." How excited we would be if we got a letter from Billy Graham, the Pope, or the head of our denomination and he called us *his friend.* Wouldn't we run to show our friends? Paul also wrote, "....and to my fellow worker," one who is equal with me, yoked together in mutual service to the Lord. Philemon was not only a *friend* but an *equal:* "...and to the church that meets in your house," where you graciously receive them all and serve as a shepherd to the flock. May the Lord give you grace, gifts, blessings, and favors. May He place peace in your heart, Philemon. How you deserve the best!

How often, when we are the one with the problem, do we begin with an uplifting thought? Aren't we more apt to throw the situation in the lap of the unsuspecting victim without as much as a hello?

> We've got a problem and it's all your fault!

> Listen, you dummy, you've done it wrong again!

> Wait till you hear what *your* son has done today!

> Because you didn't fix the faucet when I told you to do it, the whole basement is flooded!

Some of us, instead of screaming, clam up in difficult times and make others play guessing games to find out the cause of our depression.

> "What's wrong with you?"
> "Nothing."
> "There is too. You haven't said a word in ten days!"
> "Nothing is wrong."
> "Is it my mother again?"
> "No."
> "The children?"
> "No."

And on and on. We use the 20-questions approach and usually infuriate the person we should be trying to please.

When Paul faces a difficult problem, he begins with a compliment long before he even mentions the actual situation.

Concern

After the compliment he still doesn't dump the load on his friend. He next shows genuine concern.

"Brother Philemon, every time I pray, I mention you and give thanks to my God."[63]

When Paul professes that he's praying for you, he means it. He's not like some of us who promise, "I'll pray for you, honey," and then forget our pledge.

I remember a friend who called me to say she was having serious surgery. She asked if I would pray for her, and I meant to, but I went off on a trip, became involved in my ministry, and forgot poor Kitty. When I returned, she called to thank me for my prayers. How do you think I felt? There are many of us who mean well but often forget. You can't depend on us. But when Paul wrote, "Every time I pray, I pray for you," you could count on it. Not only did Paul pray, but he thanked God for his friend Philemon.

How many people do you know who pray for you daily? How many are uplifting you and praising God for your very existence? How many do you pray for consistently? Do you let them know how much you care?

Can you bring yourself to pray for problem people? Can you pray for those who've hurt you?

Paul shows genuine concern for Philemon and adds in verse 6:

> My prayer is that our fellowship with you as believers will bring about a deeper understanding of every blessing which we have in our life in union with Christ (TEV).

Paul longs for a "deeper understanding." Paul really cares, even as God cares for you and me.

Congratulations

Paul adds another positive point by showing excited appreciation for what Philemon has been doing (Verse 7):

> Your love, dear brother, has brought me great joy and much encouragement! You have cheered the hearts of all of God's people (TEV).

Paul praises him for his love, joy, encouragement, and cheer, and also for how he has spread these traits among God's people. There's no better way to keep a person's responses positive in the present problem than to remind him of how joyful he's been in the past. How few of us take the time to pave the path to the problem with praises of the person's past!

Paul has a life-or-death situation on his hands, and he skillfully and sincerely precedes his presentation with compliments, concern, and congratulations. Now for the problem.

Compromise

Because it is human nature to want to get our own way in life, we tend to use any person, title, or position we can find to wield power. When in trouble we call in our markers and hope to force a reconciliation. But note what Paul does—Paul, who personally led Philemon to the Lord, who taught him the basics of the Christian life, who is the most noted Christian leader alive at the time, who has apostolic authority available to augment his request. Paul writes in Verse 8, "I could be bold enough...to order you to do what should be done" (TEV). Don't some of us spend much of our lives working to get to a position of authority where we could legally order people to do things our way? "But love compels me to make a request instead." The love I have for you makes me want to offer a compromise instead.

> I do this even though I am Paul, the ambassador of Christ Jesus, and at present also a prisoner for his sake. So I make a request to you on behalf of Onesimus (verses 9,10 TEV).

Finally he mentions the problem: your runaway slave Onesimus. If you were Philemon, how would you react?

If I ever get my hands on the kid, I'll kill him! If he ever shows up, I'll wring his neck!

But Paul moves on quickly in verse 10: "...who is my own son in Christ; for while in prison I have become his spiritual father" (TEV). Onesimus is now a Christian, led to the Lord by Paul himself. That thought puts a different perspective on the future of Onesimus.

As if reading Philemon's mind, Paul continues in verse 11, "At one time he was of no use to you, but now he is useful both to you and to me" (TEV). Paul clearly plays on words here because Onesimus means "useful, profitable."

Now Paul states: I'll tell you what I'm going to do. I'm sending him back to you now—sending him back to be killed?—and with him goes my heart (verse 12 TEV). You mean you love him enough to put your heart on the line for a slave? "I would like to keep him here with me while I'm in prison for the gospel's sake, so that he could help me in your place" (verse 13 TEV).

I love Paul's subtle sense of humor. Not only does he tell Philemon that Onesimus is a Christian, that he is his spiritual son, that he's useful to them both, that he's sending him back with his heart, and that he'd like to keep him, but as if that is not enough, he adds, "I'd like to have him help me here in prison—in your place." These three words say, "I haven't heard much from you lately, dear friend. When I was the top traveling evangelist, you were proud to know me, but since I've been locked up, you've forgotten me. You haven't sent me any care package, no cake with a file in it, no secret plan for escape. In fact, your growing church that I helped you start hasn't even remembered its missionary commitment. Considering all that, I'd really like to keep him 'in your place.'"

Choice

"However,...." Paul, even though he has the position, doesn't tell Philemon what to do; he offers him some terms of compromise and then lets him make the choice (verse 14):

> However, I do not want to force you to help me; rather, I
> would like for you to do it of your own free will. So I will
> not do a thing unless you agree (TEV).

I'd like you to forgive the boy, welcome him home as you would welcome me, and then send him back to me with your blessing—but I won't force you. The choice is up to you. No pressure!

Challenge

So few of us have challenged people to go beyond the norm for them, but Paul is not fainthearted. He wants this problem to be solved, not at its lowest common denominator but triumphantly!

> "So if you think of me as your partner, welcome him back just as you would welcome me" (verse 17 TEV).

"Paul, what do you want from me? Isn't forgiving enough? What will people think of me making a fuss over a slave who ran away? This might start a precedent and stir unrest among the ranks. Couldn't I just keep it under wraps?"

> "If you think of me as your partner, welcome him back as you would welcome me."

How would Philemon welcome Paul? How would your church welcome Paul? Put up posters proclaiming, "I can do all things"? Take out ads in the local paper? Print announcements in the bulletin? Create buttons with Paul's picture?

> "Welcome him as you would welcome me."

What a challenge to rise above the mediocre of life and celebrate over a little black sheep who was lost and is now found!

Then Paul adds another touch of humor in verse 18: "If he has done you any wrong or owes you anything, charge it to my account" (TEV).

In case Philemon is held back by a desire for restitution, Paul lets him know he can charge it on his Visa card. Can you imagine what Paul's credit rating was as he sat chained to a guard in prison? But Paul had learned to keep life in perspective, and he could have a light touch even in heavy circumstances.

"Here, I will write this with my own hand: *I, Paul, will pay you back*" (verse 19 TEV). Then in case Philemon wonders where or with what, Paul adds, "I should not have to remind you, of course, that you owe your very life to me" (verse 19b TEV). "So if you never get a nickel out of me, consider what your life is worth." Paul doesn't rub it in; he doesn't say, "I made you what you are today"—as we might be apt to make clear—he just lets him know, "I'm willing to pay, but if I can't, remember, you owe your very life to me." Then he adds, "So, my brother, please do me this favor for the Lord's sake; as a brother in Christ, cheer me up!" (verse 20 TEV).

If you wish to cheer me up, don't send ornate greeting cards or cable flowers—just welcome Onesimus as you would welcome me. That's all I ask, and I challenge you to do it.

Confidence

There's no better way to seal an agreement than to let the person know you have confidence in his attitude and his wisdom. What uplifting words Paul pens!

> I am sure, as I write this, that you will do what I ask—in fact I know that you will do even more (verse 21 TEV).

What encouraging words Paul uses—"I'm sure" and "I know"! So many of us go through life hearing about what we're incompetent to handle. "You've never been able to..." "There's no hope that you'll ever..." "You've always done it wrong..." "Why can't you be smart like...?"

How quickly we are drawn to the person who says, "I have confidence in you—I know I can count on you."

In case confidence doesn't hit the mark, Paul adds a clincher: "At the same time, get a room ready for me" (verse 22 TEV). I'm planning to spring out of here any minute to catch the next plane and be at the celebration myself.

And then in case the church has been negligent in upholding Paul in their prayers, he stirs them up by his confidence in their spirituality: "I hope that God will answer the prayers of all of you and give me back to you....May the grace of the Lord Jesus Christ be with you all" (verses 22, 25 TEV).

What a beautiful letter! How Paul has learned through being humbled and dragged through adverse circumstances to praise the Lord and deal nicely with difficult people!

Conclusion

History tells us that Philemon accepted Onesimus back and forgave him, that the church dedicated him as a helper to Paul, and that later Onesimus became the bishop of Ephesus.

How many of us are willing to put our pride in our pocket and go out on a limb for a friend? How many times have we avoided taking a chance or putting our reputation on the line, and not helped a person in need? How many people—your friends, your mates, your children—are waiting for encouragement from you, an uplifting word of confidence that might change the direction of their lives?

Do you have:

- A child who needs a challenge?

- A friend who has no future?

- A boy who could be a bishop?

Chapter 6

How Can We Handle
a Difficult Situation?

We all want to know how to get along with difficult people. Dale Carnegie's *How to Win Friends and Influence People* is the all-time bestseller in this field. Today personality-improvement courses abound on every corner, and the seminar business is spreading like the measles. Are there any new tricks? Is there any painless, effortless way to make getting along any easier? Can we slip happiness pills to the negative thinkers? Is there a big bottle of ink eradicator to pour over those we'd like to eliminate, or some white-out to paint over black clouds? Would Superman please come to the rescue?

We all want the easy way, but there's no magic formula without effort. Paul had to learn how to handle difficult situations, and we can learn from him. We've seen what his letter to Philemon said and meant; now how does it apply to us?

Compliments

Even though Paul thought of it first, Carnegie's basic principle for winning friends is to give compliments, to find something genuinely good in everyone. This is not doing what comes naturally, because we all tend to knock other people to make ourselves look good. As Christians we like to call our observations of the negative in other people a "discerning spirit, a true gift from the Lord." If you really are a designated discerner, God won't let your talent go unnoticed. He will send people in need to your door, inspire you to write positive passages, and place you on *Oprah.*

If these adventures haven't come to you, perhaps your ability to judge is not a spiritual gift, and you might try to make the giving of compliments a new goal in your life.

Years ago when I taught elementary psychology to adults, I assigned my students to give genuine compliments for a week. I suggested that they look around for people in need of praise and find something sincere to say.

A nurse reported at our next session that twice a week a little old man came to the office for shots. He would be outside waiting each morning when she would arrive, and she would pass him by with a nod.

When 9 o'clock came she would let him in from the cold, give him his shot, and dismiss him. After our assignment, she noticed him the next morning and wondered what she could find about him to compliment. As she glanced his way, she saw he was wearing a bright red tie with a palm tree painted on it. She smiled and asked, "Is that a new tie you have on, Mr. Costello? That palm tree is a beauty!"

He nodded as she went quickly inside. A few minutes later she thought, "Why do I let that little man stand out in the cold? I could let him in to wait." She called to him, and he entered thankfully.

Two days later when she came to work, he was standing proudly at the door with a dozen roses in his hands. "These are for you because you were so kind to me. My son sent me that tie from Palm Springs, and you're the only one who's noticed."

A young man lived with his brothers and widowed father. His one sister kept house for them all, and her services were taken for granted. Because of his assignment, he looked around at home for something to compliment and noticed some new flowered drapes. He told her how beautiful they were, and she replied, "I'm glad someone finally noticed. I made them months ago, and I felt none of you even cared. You're the only one who's noticed." The next day when he came home from work, there was a new sweater on his bed with a note: "Because you noticed."

To compliment we first have to "notice." We have to open our preoccupied minds and take the blinders off our glazed eyes. From the time I taught this class and heard the amazing reports from the students, I put myself on a compliment course. As Marita and I travel, we look for people who could use encouragement. One day I noticed a lady in line at the ticket counter at Los Angeles Airport who had on an ordinary house dress and was carrying a shopping bag. As I glanced her way, I saw she had silver-etched, heart-shaped buttons down the front of the dress. "What beautiful buttons you have!" I commented. She looked up and beamed.

"My friend brought these home from Germany, and I made the whole dress to go with the buttons. You're the first one who's noticed them."

Start today on a compliment course. Practice on everyone you meet. You can always praise the buttons. Be the first one to notice what's good. "If there be any virtue, and if there be any praise, think [and comment] on these things."[64]

As I've taught the button principle in seminars, it has caught on, and often I meet someone who remembers, smiles at me and says, "My, you have beautiful buttons." Practice noticing and praising, for there are very few people in life who have really lost all their buttons.

How do you, like Paul, use compliments to deal with difficult situations? Think now of some person who troubles you much. The next time you see that body heading your way, look for the buttons. Quickly find something genuinely positive to compliment. It's hard for that person to tackle you when you've started on a gracious note.

How about your husband? What do other women notice about him? Have you told him lately that you love him? How about your wife? Do you compliment her cooking? If you don't, she might quit and let you get your own dinner.

How about your teenager? So many feel their parents haven't said a kind word to them in years! Compliment their friends for something. They all have buttons! I came home one day to find a shabbily dressed teen sprawled on my couch. He was young Fred's friend, and I wanted to say something nice. As he stood up to greet me, he straightened out his layered T-shirts and pulled up his sagging shorts.

All I could think of to say was "You look so relaxed in those clothes."

He winked and said to me, "I go for the low-maintenance look." Later he told Fred, "Your mother likes my style."

As I shared this point one day with Dr. Starr, my nutritionist, she looked reflective and said, "That's what my daughter is looking for—some praise from me. I've paid for her training as a classical pianist, and all she wants to play is jazz. Each time she sits at the piano to play, I suggest Beethoven and she responds with jazz. I sigh and turn away. Now I see I must encourage her even if her music is not my choice."

So many of us parents are not complimenting our children on what they're doing well, because it isn't what we had in mind for them to do. They either become discouraged and quit or find someone else who will appreciate their abilities.

One day when Marita was in her twenties, she returned from a few days in a friend's home. As we discussed her time there, she said, "There's something not quite right about that family. I don't know what it is, but I felt a tension in the home." We talked over the possibilities and then it clicked. "No one ever gave compliments to anyone else. When the mother put dinner on the table, the kids complained, and the father didn't stop them." A home with no compliments is not a happy place, and it's up to the parents to set the tone.

I remember when we were getting ready to move, and I had hastily thrown together an unnamed casserole from an odd assortment of leftovers. Young Fred, who was a teenager at the time, looked at the mound on his plate and exclaimed, "What in the world do you call this?"

His father countered, "Be grateful your mother came home and cooked anything, and eat it gladly."

Fred smiled weakly up at me and said, "Sure is a nice dinner, Mom."

When we as parents use compliments as the norm, we give our home a warm, positive atmosphere and set the stage for a loving home life in our children's future. They learn from what we do, not from what we say.

How do compliments help in your social life or business? In any position of leadership, we run into people who don't see things our way. Our human tendency is to try to convince them we're right, but when we're willing to praise them and make them look good in front of other people, they often become supportive. As I have been president of different organizations, I've found many women whose sole joy in life was scuttling the president's plans. I've always gone out of my way to compliment them in person. "Why, that's a brilliant idea! There's not one of us here who couldn't profit from your suggestion."

Even more effective is quietly saying positive words "behind their backs." To Mabel's friend, "Have you ever noticed how agreeable Mabel is? She always wants what's best for the club, and I appreciate that attitude." The friend may be stunned at the thought of Mabel being agreeable, but she'll tell her about it within minutes.

I always personally read the evaluation sheets we get in from our CLASS seminars. One lady wrote an extra note to me expressing her discontent with one of the leaders. Everyone else had written praises for the same person, so I could have ignored the comment. As I thought about it, I decided to call her in another state and thank her for caring enough to write me the note. She was stunned to hear from me, and as we conversed she felt better about the situation and said she guessed she had been in a bad mood that day. When we take a positive approach to a negative situation, there can be amazing results.

As we drove in toward a church in Dallas where I was having a seminar, the hostess said to me, "I hate to tell you this, but not many people are coming tonight. I cleared this program with the pastor, but I didn't know I should have checked it with Dolores. She doesn't really have a title, but she is constantly making coffee for the pastor, cleaning up the church, and I found out that through the years she has unofficially had the final word on all the women's activities. She's offended that I didn't know her position, and she's called the church women and told them not to come. It's got nothing to do with you personally."

I was glad for that at least. I tried not to show my disappointment, and I pledged to share my message with whatever ones appeared. We entered the foyer, and the hostess left me to go and find the pastor.

As I looked around, I noticed a woman in the sanctuary polishing the pews with Liquid Gold. She had on a print house dress with a different print apron, plus stockings rolled down around her ankles, and she was astride a basketful of cleaning supplies. I took a chance that this was Dolores. I walked down the aisle behind her and startled her with, "Are you by any chance Dolores?" She turned quickly, the ring of keys on her belt clanking against each other as she looked me over. Since my picture was on posters in the foyer, I assumed she could guess who I was.

"How did you know?" she asked suspiciously.

"I've spoken in many churches in this town, and they all wish they had someone like Dolores, someone who really cares for their church like you do for this one."

She smiled slightly on one side of her face and then shot another squirt of Liquid Gold on the pew. I told her my name and gave her the news that I was doing a seminar in this very room tonight. I thanked her for caring enough to polish the pews for me and then asked her a favor.

"When I go into a church, I need to find a responsible person who can assist me and pass out my outlines at the right time. Since I don't know a soul here and you are obviously someone I could count on, I wonder if you'd be willing to help me out?"

Before she had a chance to say no, I asked if she could call a few friends to assist her and be available 15 minutes early for my instructions. I thanked her again for her industry, patted her on the shoulder, and said I'd see her later.

What did Dolores do the rest of the afternoon? She called her friends, and I had the biggest group of ushers I'd ever had!

When you have a human-relations problem, don't run away or weep and wail. Tackle the situation quickly, get to the source of the problem, praise the person for whatever you can find, and let him know you have confidence in him.

Difficult people need loving too!

Concern

Dale Carnegie once said, "You can make more friends in two months by becoming interested in other people than you can in two years by trying to get other people interested in you."

So many of our humanistic self-help programs today work on an opposite principle: that to get people to like you, you must be worldly-wise and slim to the point of being anorexic. You must have shiny hair that bounces as you run through meadows full of poppies, and perfume so magnetic that it will draw handsome men from miles away. A powerful personality may be appealing for the moment, but for a lasting relationship nothing beats a genuine concern for the welfare of other people.

As a speaker I spend my time ministering to the needs of others, so it is memorable when someone from the audience seeks me out to show concern for me. Many years ago in Tucson, Arizona, Barbara Tompkins asked if there was something she could pray for in my life. She knew I had lost two brain-damaged sons, so when I mentioned that my daughter Lauren was pregnant with my first grandchild, she knew of my concern. I explained that my boys had appeared normal until they were six months old, and so I wouldn't know even at birth if my new grandchild would be normal. Barbara hugged me warmly and promised that she and Janie would pray for me each Wednesday when they met for lunch.

Within a week of that time, I was speaking in Walnut Creek, and Oralyn Denison, the chairman, asked if there was any prayer request I had, for she felt led to pray for me. Again I explained the situation, and she promised she would pray.

James Randall Briggs Jr. was born on February 27, 1978. He appeared healthy and normal, but Lauren and I watched him carefully. About a week after he was six months old, I got a letter from Barbara in Tucson. She affirmed that she had met each Wednesday for lunch with Janie and that they had prayed consistently for my Randy. The same day I got the letter from Barbara, I received a phone call from Oralyn. "Ever since you were here, my Bible study and I have prayed each Friday morning for your grandchild. We assume he must be about six months old now, and we want to know how he's doing."

I'll never forget Barbara and Oralyn, two very busy ladies who took time to show genuine concern for me. I don't care if their hair is bouncy, if they're slim or if they wear the right perfume. I only care that they cared for me.

When Barbara Bueler lost her home and all her possessions in the Panorama Fire that swept through Southern California, many friends expressed verbal concern. The community asked for clothing to be donated for the victims, and Barbara received three Hefty bags full. When she took the garments out of the bags, she found many where the owner had cut off the buttons (nothing left to compliment) or where zippers had been ripped out, leaving gaping holes. Some dresses had miniskirts and styles that were passé. The people meant well and had collected their tax-deductible receipts, but they had given from their rejects and not from their hearts. If you wouldn't wear it yourself, why would you give it to someone else?

It's not easy to show genuine concern for other people. Our basic instinct for self-preservation keeps us from wanting to get involved with the problems of others. "I've got my own problems," we say, and surely we do.

But we must make a basic decision: Do we want to withdraw from the reality of the chaos around us, to protect our emotions, and to live a pleasant, plastic life, or are we willing to be vulnerable, to look into the hurting hearts and feel their pain? This caring approach is neither easy nor popular.

As my daughter Lauren has conducted interviews for her book *I Don't Know What to Say,* she has found that women sense when friends are hurting but they choose to look the other way. They might send a card or donate money, but they don't want to get involved.

Lloyd John Ogilvie, while pastor of Hollywood Presbyterian Church, asked his TV audiences over the years to send in their deepest needs so that he could speak to them. He's asked, "What do you need humanly and spiritually?" In his book *Freedom of the Spirit,* he reports that in all the answers he's received, no one has ever said that his deepest need was to become a servant, to be more giving.

Humanly speaking, it's not an attractive aim, but aren't we to be different from the world? Isn't the Christian to have the attitude of Christ Jesus, who took on the nature of a servant, who was humbled and walked the path of obedience?[65]

If we really want to get along with other people, we don't need to worry about our externals—we have to rededicate our *internals* to showing genuine concern for others. I've met many beautiful people in my lifetime, and I'm always attracted to those who are well put together and have charm and wit, but I will never forget:

> *Barbara* and *Oralyn,* who prayed without ceasing for my grandson.

Emilie Barnes, who invites Fred and me for a gourmet dinner and the next day sends me a thank-you note for coming.

Lucy Tulanian, who writes me notes and cards of encouragement several times a month.

Marilyn Murray, who took me into her home, let me write parts of two books there, loved me, and cared for me—all when she was in excruciating pain herself.

Kitty Reynolds, my deceased friend, who truly had the heart of a servant, who came early to my house to set up at all my social events, and who always stayed to help with the dishes.

Lorna Farthing, who came daily to care for me when I was ill, who stood at my side to assist me at the Women's Club, and who has been my devoted best friend for 30 years.

Betty Lou Whittemore, who visited my dying mother weekly, who brought her little gifts, and who stood in for me when I was out of town.

All those friends who, when hearing that Fred had a business crisis, wrote and said, "We don't need to know the details—we just want to tell you we're praying for you and we really care!"

They have a place in my Forever Hall of Fame, not because of their looks or charm but because I know they care for me. Their actions speak louder than words.

Why don't you make a list of those people who have cared for you at some point in your life, those who have shown genuine concern for you, those with the attitude of a servant?

What consistency do you find in their actions?

In their attitudes?

Now make a list of the selfless, caring deeds you've done for others.

How about those you thought about but never quite got to doing?

Now list some of the difficult people you have to deal with.

Do they know you really care for them?
Have you told them lately that you love them?
Have you found out what's really causing their pain?
Have you given them a non-threatening time to share their problems with you?
Have you written them a note, sent a card, given a gift?

Difficult people are always hurting inside, but they cover it up by being rude, defensive, or withdrawn. Don't accept them at face value, but instead be the one who takes the time to show genuine concern.

Congratulations

Have you ever watched one of those game shows where someone is about to win a prize? There's an air of excitement. Someone's going to be a winner!

Do you remember watching Richard Dawson kiss all those ladies on *Family Feud?* They knew they'd never see him again, but they loved every minute of it. He made them feel good. While he didn't appeal to me as he fawned over the females, we *can* learn a lesson from him. He could go up to a little ordinary lady, kiss her and tell her she was beautiful, and right before your eyes she would transform.

It was like waving a magic wand over Cinderella. Whether he told the truth or not didn't seem to matter. When he proclaimed her a winner, she became a *winner!*

Even the mere chance of winning motivates people to action. The Women's Club keeps its chairwomen motivated all year for the chance of winning a district award. They'll drag floral displays to the Orange Show in hope of a five-cent blue ribbon, they'll bake cakes for the contest, and they'll stand with wild anticipation while the judges taste and test.

Have you ever observed women at a luncheon, clutching little numbered tickets, waiting to win a door prize? They know the items are all rejects from their friends, "white elephants" that no one wants; yet they scream when their number's called and gasp with delight as they unwrap three-legged plastic dogs with rhinestone eyes.

Why will we work so hard for so little, or get so excited over something so insignificant? Because we all want to be winners. We all want to be queen for a day. We all long to hear those words, "Congratulations, you're a winner!"

If we accept that everyone wants to be a winner and that we want to get along better with people, what obvious tool is laid before us? If we can make people feel like winners, we'll be loved by all.

William James, the honored philosopher, once said, "The deepest principle in human nature is the craving to be appreciated."

One day as I was checking out of the Hilton in Eugene, Oregon, the young bell man named Sean helped me with my bags. When he asked where I was going I responded, "To the coast to write a book."

"What's the name of it?" he asked.

"How to Get Along with Difficult People."

"Boy, do I get a lot of them!"

"Sean, what would be your definition of a difficult person?"

He thought for a few seconds and then replied, "People that, no matter how hard you try to please them or how much you do for them, never appreciate your efforts."

People who don't feel good about themselves have difficulty saying thank you. Eventually they become difficult and bitter. What can we do to prevent this from happening and to repair the present damage?

We can say thank you to others and then congratulate instead of criticize.

Years ago when Marita left for college, young Fred said to me, "I guess it's going to be dull around here for you without Marita. She's the one who makes you laugh."

I thought about that comment and realized I had communicated to him that to get Mother's approval you had to be funny. For me to tell him that wasn't so wouldn't change his mind, so I began to listen for light comments he might make. With Marita gone he began to talk more, and when he said anything remotely humorous, I would laugh and commend him. He may never be a comedian, but he's loosened up a lot as I've congratulated him.

Praise for humor may not be what your son needs, but there's some area in which he'd like to be a winner. Find it and fill it!

How about your husband? How often do you congratulate him for anything? When he comes home at night, he needs a blue ribbon for something. Either he's had a terrible day or he's been flattered by the women at work—and you come across as a dismal contrast. In either case, he wants to know that *you* think he's a winner.

How about your father-in-law? You say he's never smiled, and the Lord Himself couldn't please him.

What a challenge! Find some way you can congratulate him. He may never give you credit for your positive attitude, but behind your back he'll say to his cronies, "You know, she's not all bad."

How about your mother? One lady at CLASS came to me in tears about her mother. She lived with her, and according to her mother's comments, she had never done anything right. "Just last night I had company and prepared a gourmet dinner. At the end, as others thanked me, she said, 'The next time you make this, use a little less salt.' I felt like hitting her!"

Using our CLASS principle, "Every bad experience is a good example," I suggested that she keep a list of these "delightful" examples her mother provided for a future talk on dealing with the elderly. I hadn't intended that she tell her mother, but the next day she reported that when her mother had been critical that night she thanked her. Her mother asked why she thanked her, and she told her she was keeping a list of her humorous examples for a book she was going to write. Amazingly, the mother was flattered that her words were quotable and that she might be in a book. By the end of the evening when she would drop a caustic comment, she would giggle and say, "There's another good example; did you write it down?"

The more critical a person is, the more desperate is his craving for appreciation.

How about your pastor? He came out of a seminary with a brilliant knowledge of Greek and a commission to exegete, but he's found a flock that's all Greek to him and that thinks exegesis is a dirty word. He's been told what's wrong with him, with his wife, and with his children, and he feels his deep truths have fallen on shallow ears. He needs to win some kind of prize. Be creative!

Why is there an epidemic of teenage suicide in this country? Why was Plano, Texas—a model community outside Dallas—named the teen suicide capital?

Why did two of my son's friends kill themselves in their senior year at Redlands High? When I asked him about this, he said "Most of my friends don't see much hope for the future."

I explained that as Christians we have an eternal hope even when today seems hopeless. God does have a plan for each of our lives, and we defy God when we take our lives away from His control. I suggested that he help his friends find purpose in life and not contribute to their general depression.

There are hurting teenagers everywhere we look. Some of them might be yours. Some might be your neighbors or your grandchildren, or teens in your church youth group. Do you notice troubled teens? Do you try to uplift them? Do you notice anything they do right and congratulate them? Do you give them hope?

The *Today* show did a series on teen suicides. One pretty girl of 14 told the story of why she tried to kill herself. "Nobody loves me, and I don't see that things are going to change much." Her mother came on to say she had no idea the girl felt that way until she'd found her drugged in the bathroom.

Psychiatrist Steven Shelov came on to say that teens are crying out for love and attention but parents are too busy to hear their cries. Divorces rock the security of the children and give them a feeling that no one loves them, even though parents may be outdoing themselves in giving gifts and favors. He stated that 80 percent of the suicides, or suicide attempts, are by children of broken homes where they do not live with both natural parents. They may be in a one-parent home or a step-family situation. No matter how well the parents do in these cases, the teens often feel rejected, unloved, like losers.

Difficult people feel like losers, but they really want to be winners. Could you offer some kind of congratulations?

Compromise

Compromise means "promise together, make a mutual pledge, come in from the extremes and meet on a common ground." World powers have to compromise to coexist. Management and labor have to hammer out compromise agreements to keep functioning. Compromise is a proven tool in getting along with difficult people, and yet as individuals we resist using it because underneath we'd really like to have our own way.

Think of some person with whom you have a problem right now. Is there some concession you could offer that you haven't been willing to give in the past? Could you move across the center barrier onto their side? I know they don't deserve it—and yes, you might lose face—but remember the Lord's own words: "Blessed are the peacemakers: for they shall be called the children of God."[66]

When Marita was 13, it was the era of tie-dyed T-shirts and frayed jeans. Even though I had grown up in the Depression with no money for clothes, I had never dressed so poorly. Marita had a closet full of ruffled dresses I had bought her, but she would gag when I tried to get one on her. One day I saw her out in the driveway rubbing the hems of her new jeans with dirt and rocks. I was aghast at her ruining these expensive pants I had just paid for and ran out to tell her so. She continued to grind on as I recounted my soap opera of childhood deprivation.

As I concluded without having moved her to tears of repentance, I asked why she was wrecking her new jeans. She replied without looking up, "You can't wear new ones."

"Why not?"

"You just can't, so I'm messing them up to make them look old." Such total loss of logic! How could it be the style to ruin new clothes?

Each morning as she would leave for school, I would stare at her and sigh, "My daughter looking like that." There she'd stand in her father's old T-shirt, tie-dyed with big blue spots and streaks. Fit for a duster, I thought. And those jeans—so low-slung I feared if she raised her arms they'd drop off her rear. But where would they go? I held that fear until one day I saw in the corner of Marita's room that same pair of jeans standing up alone. They were so stiff they weren't dropping anywhere. They didn't need Marita inside them for strength, but when she did wear them, the frayed bottoms, helped by the rocks, had strings, almost fringes, that dragged behind her, gathering up dirt, gum wrappers, and dead insects.

One day after she left for school, it was as if the Lord got my attention and said, "Do you realize what your last words are to Marita each morning? 'My daughter looking like that.' When she gets to school and her friends talk about their old-fashioned mothers who complain all the time, she'll have your constant comments to contribute." I could just see her in a dramatic pose giving a Hamlet-like soliloquy, "You should hear *my* mother! She goes on about her poverty during childhood and then moans 'My child, looking like that!'" Her friends would applaud. They all thought she was adorable. I was the lone dissenter.

As I thought the matter over, I wondered what the other teens looked like. I drove over to pick her up that day, and as the junior high girls poured out onto the sidewalk, they all looked like assorted sizes of Marita. In fact, many of the girls looked worse. On the way home, I mentioned how I had overreacted to her ruining her jeans. I offered a compromise: "From now on you can wear anything you want to school and with your friends, and I won't say a word about it."

"That'll be the day!"

"But your part is when I take you out with me to church or shopping or to my friends', you dress in something you know I like without my having to say a word."

She thought about it.

Then I added, "That means you get 95 percent your way and I get 5 percent for me. What do you think?"

She got a twinkle in her eye as she put out her skinny little hand and shook mine. "Mother, you've got yourself a deal!"

From then on I gave her a happy farewell in the morning and didn't bug her about her clothes. When I took her out with me, she dressed properly without fussing. We had ourselves a deal!

Within the year she went from those huge, ugly T-shirts to pretty ones, and the next year into blouses, sweaters, and skirts. By her senior year in high school, she was wearing expensive dresses and high heels, and one day I heard myself say, "Marita, those clothes are too good to wear to school!"

Are we mothers ever satisfied? No wonder our children are confused. I'm grateful I compromised with Marita because if I'd continued to carry on about her clothes she might still be tie-dyed today.

There comes a time when our children are grown enough that we can allow them more flexibility than we have in the past. As Paul says, "I could be bold enough to tell you what to do, but because I love you, I'll make a request instead."

Requests versus orders are difficult for a Choleric parent to make, but we can learn. We want everyone to do it our way—now! But we have to ask ourselves, in the long run does it make that much of a difference? Is *later* that much worse than now? I remember back when our son, Fred, was about 20. He was working but living at home, and he was capable of handling his own life and making his own decisions. One day, as the eternal mother, I did Fred's laundry for him. He could do it perfectly well by himself, but I decided to go the extra mile, knowing how grateful he'd be for my sacrificial act. As I hung the last of ten shirts on a rod over the dryer in the garage, the door went up, and Fred drove in beside me. As I pointed to the shirts all in a row, I said joyfully, "Look what Mother's done for you!"

"Noble, Mother," he replied, and headed for the house. That wasn't the reaction I'd expected, so I went on.

"Fred, since I've done all this work, I'd like you to take these shirts to your room."

Any mother alive would agree that was a reasonable request. Fred answered, "Not now, I have something else in mind."

"Something else in mind?" I thought (but didn't say). To myself I mumbled, "I didn't ask you what *you* wanted to do. I told you to take the shirts to your room. After all I've done for you, it's the least you could do for me!"

Fortunately, as these thoughts went through my mind, I had time to swallow and respond, "That's fine, Fred. Whenever you have time."

He left, and I stood there amazed that I had been able to compromise on my request.

As I thought about it, I realized it doesn't really matter when Fred takes his shirts to his room—in fact, it wouldn't make much difference if he never took them to his room. Would it ruin my life if he lived in the garage with his shirts?

When I tell this story at a seminar, I have mothers come up and thank me for the example, saying they are still yelling at their children for inconsequential trivia. One lady said, "I get furious at my son whenever he doesn't do what I want right off. Just yesterday I called out, 'I didn't ask you if you wanted to—I just told you to do it.' I didn't realize how bad I sounded until you said those words on stage; no wonder he doesn't want to be with me."

Sometimes we create our own special difficult people by insisting that they do it our way *now.*

A spirit of compromise softens hard people.

Choice

"However," Paul says, "I don't want to force you. I'd rather you did it of your own free will."

Difficult people don't like being forced into anything; they like to do it of their own free will.

With a little creative thought, it's amazing how easy it is to make your will their will. In women's club or church work, difficult people flourish as predictably as mildew creeps into a pile of damp towels. If they find out what the leader wants, they'll vote no. How do you handle groups of difficult people like those in the Big Brown Church on the Move?

First, you let them know that you are there as their servant. You emphasize that you will take no sides on issues and that your will is second to the will of the group. They are so used to domineering leadership that this will brand you immediately as different in a positive way.

Back when I was in what my children called Mother's Presidential Era, I always tried to explain to the women the pros and cons of each issue and then mention again, "The choice is up to you." I would then open it up for discussion without trying to make them see it my way. I've found from years of experience that whichever side stands up first with a persuasive point of view seems to influence the vote. If it was an issue I really cared strongly about, I would prearrange for a lady on that side to stand up the minute I opened the discussion. This put the other side on the defensive, a position that seldom leads to victory. You can give the group a choice and still win.

What about with children? As mine were growing up, I explained the roles we all had in keeping the home going. Father worked to support us while I cooked, cleaned, entertained, and supervised the children. They did certain chores as their part of the household responsibilities and lived according to the rules. We set the rules at family meetings, where their opinions were asked about bed hours, allowances, visitors, vacations, and other pertinent areas. They were a part of setting up the rules;

they had a choice. I made out a family work chart, and they had to have their week's duties done before they could go out of the house on Saturday. I didn't care when they did them; they had a choice within a time frame.

One boy who visited with us for a week said to young Fred, "Your mother must really like me. She put me on the work chart."

Part of helping your children to mature is allowing them to make more major choices as they get older.

When Fred was 15, he announced that he wanted to buy a motorcycle with his own money. There's probably few of you mothers reading this who would get excited over your teenage son wanting to buy a motorcycle, especially after all you've spent at the orthodontist! I had never understood why in California a child could get a permit to drive a motorcycle out on the freeway at 15 but he had to wait until he was 16 to pilot a sturdy sedan. Father Fred set a time for our cycle conference, as we made pro-and-con lists. We had all the cons:

> WE: You won't want to ride it when it rains.
> FRED: I love a motorcycle in the rain. I love the feel of the rain rushing through my hair.

> WE: As soon as you turn 16, you'll want to borrow a car for dates.
> FRED: I'll only date girls who like to ride on motorcycles. (What a terrible thought! I pictured him tooling up the drive, bringing home some Amazon wearing a black leather jacket and a helmet.)

> WE: When you want to buy a car, you'll never be able to get your money out of the motorcycle.
> FRED: You can always sell a bike for more than you paid for it.

We went over all of our ideas and then let him know if he bought the cycle he could not borrow the car, nor would we buy him one. After much discussion, we let him make the choice. I wish I could say our brilliance swayed him, but it didn't. He chose to buy the cycle. We didn't nag him about it; we just accepted his choice.

When fall came it started to rain. One day he stormed in, helmet in hand, and exclaimed, "I hate riding this thing in the rain!"

Like any normal mother, I couldn't resist saying, "No, no, Fred. Don't you remember? You love the motorcycle in the rain, the feel of the rain rushing through your hair."

He was now 16 and wanted to take a special girl to a party. He asked to borrow our car. "Oh no," I dramatized. "You only date girls who like motorcycles."

"Well, this one doesn't," he explained.

Was I glad! We didn't give him the car, and the girl's mother drove them. "It was a humiliating experience," he told us.

Finally one rainy Saturday night, Fred walked into the kitchen, slammed down his wet helmet and said, "Okay, you've won!"

"Won what, Fred?"

"I'm sick of this bike."

Naturally, I had to say, "Well, you have nothing to worry about, since you can always sell it for more than you paid for it." But Fred couldn't sell it for any price.

We allowed Fred to make a choice, and he learned to regret it. He has never wanted a motorcycle again.

Please realize that I'm not telling you to let your sons have motorcycles; I'm just teaching the principle that sooner or later we have to let our children make decisions that may not be the best. We show them each side and let them make the choice.

I talk to many women who have husbands in mid-life crises buying motorcycles or other toys. They weren't allowed this selection as youths, and they're making immature choices now.

Difficult people rebel under a dictatorship, but given an occasional choice, they feel important and will respond in a positive way. Making choices and being forced to live with the consequences (rather than being bailed out by Mother or Father) is a key element in growing up.

Challenge

In *Blow Away the Black Clouds* I state, "No goal=no achieve-ment=depression." Many people become difficult because they see no future, no hope. They're not heading anywhere, so they're not going to get there. Sometimes they have no money, and that further discourages them from trying.

I remember the lady who looked at my two brothers and me as children and said, "It's a shame there's no hope for them, as they seem so bright." We all decided right then, "We'll show her!" She became a challenge to us even though that was not her intention. Had we been Phlegmatic, we might have given up, or if Melancholy, we would have been depressed, but our Choleric determination wanted to prove that we could do the impossible. The impossible just takes a little longer!

My father and mother both encouraged us, and even though we had to study on a table in our store while the customers watched, our parents watched what we were doing and kept moving us along.

Many of our youthful challenges were caused by lack of money. We knew we had to make it on our own and we all determined to become successful. I didn't care how hard I had to work as long as I could get through college and become a teacher. Jim worked his way through college and seminary and earned two bachelor's degrees and two master's degrees. Ron has become an outstanding radio personality, and he has been number 1 out of all the stations in Dallas for about 30 years. We look back and are grateful that our parents encouraged us to press on and not give up because of our circumstances. In 1980 I felt a call of the Lord to challenge Christians who had some-thing to say but didn't know how to say it. I started CLASS (Chris-tian Leaders, Authors & Speakers Seminars) to train potential speakers and challenge would-be writers. It is so easy in our busy society to keep occupied and yet accomplish nothing of eternal significance. Charlie Jarvis once said, "We're so busy being good, we have no time to be excellent."

As we train men and women to be alert to life, to notice what's going on around them, to be sensitive to people's needs, to think on more than one track at a time, we see people blossom. At the end of three days, many of them say, "I've never been so challenged before. I know my life will never be the same."

Paul challenged Philemon to stretch, to go beyond what was natural. He asked him to accept Onesimus back not as a slave but as a brother in Christ. More than that, he prodded him to treat Onesimus as he would treat Paul himself if he returned.

I'm sure Philemon asked himself, "Can I do that?"

Can all of us stretch beyond what's comfortable?

If you're not doing something that frightens you a bit, you're not living up to your potential. In recent years assorted studies have shown that we can prevent senility if we keep our minds active. Each time we put new information into our brains, our minds improve. It's always easier as we grow older to coast, to watch mindless TV, or to read pleasant but unchallenging books. But the studies show that putting new material into our minds is what makes the difference: new languages, new instruction, new hobbies, new research, new classes.

In our society we have continually downgraded the elderly and given glory to the young—to the ultimate benefit of neither. Many women I talk with have difficult elderly mothers who have been shoved away and are constantly complaining. Wouldn't every one of us be difficult if we were put somewhere to sit and told it's all downhill from here?

Minds of all ages need challenges; if we could find purposeful activities for our seniors, they wouldn't be so difficult. I read the results of a test done on rats to determine what causes senility. They put two groups of rats in different cages. They all got equal food and care, but one group had new toys put into the cage each day and the other group had no toys. Those with fresh challenges kept alert while the other rats ceased using their brains and became senile. What a challenge for our churches to have meaningful programs for the elderly!

My mother's church in Westfield, Massachusetts, did an exceptional job with its seniors. Each Sunday a member would pick my mother up and take her to church and the coffee hour that followed. On Wednesdays a group called "Gift Shop" got together to work on craft items for the yearly Christmas Bazaar. They were given instructions and sent home to produce some item which would ultimately be sold to help pay off the mortgage. Mother loved "Gift Shop" because she was challenged to do something for a worthy cause. Each senior worked hard at home to bring in the most items the next week.

Once a month her group put on a supper, and Mother would spend the day peeling potatoes. Everyone was encouraged in whatever job she did, and when Mother moved to be with us in California, the group gave her a gilded peeler on a plaque labeled "The Golden Peeler Award." She treasured that plaque.

Whether you have trouble with a teen, a friend, or a mother, think of ways to give that person something significant to live for. Give them a challenge, some new hope, and they won't be so difficult any longer.

NO GOAL = NO ACHIEVEMENT = *DEPRESSION!*

Confidence

We've all heard of governments that were brought to collapse by a "no confidence" vote, and yet few of us realize that we are voting "no confidence" in other people daily.

We tell our husbands:

> You've failed again.
> You'll never repair that.
> You must be color-blind.
> You never smile anymore.
> *Votes of No Confidence!*

We tell our children:

> You never help me.
> Your room's always a mess.

> Your hair is disgusting.
> Your clothes are a fright.
> *Votes of No Confidence!*

We tell our groups:

> This will never work out.
> No one will ever notice all we've done.
> Last year's chairman had a nervous breakdown.
> Why don't we all just quit?
> *Votes of No Confidence!*

We tell our employees:

> I don't want any excuses; just do it.
> Don't tell me your troubles.
> I fired the last person who said that.
> I knew you couldn't do it.
> *Votes of No Confidence!*

The world is full of people who are voting "no confidence" in others. These are difficult people who set themselves as judges over all the other difficult people who are in every family, every business, and every church.

How can we be different? We can instill confidence in others, raise their self-image, and increase their productivity.

Confidence means a state of trust, reliance, and assurance. "I believe in you; I can rely on you; I *know* I can count on you." Paul tells Philemon, "I am *sure* you will do as I ask. I *know* you will do even more."

In a society of put-downs, we all need to have someone who believes in us. People in mid-life crises think no one has confidence in them, including themselves. They're strangely driven to do things they never planned on doing in order to prove to themselves that they have some worth.

Fred told me during a time of business problems, "If you'll just believe in me, I know I can make it." We all need to know that someone believes in us. How can this knowledge help us to get along with other people? As we stated earlier in this book, we should find other people's needs and then fill them. If we all need someone who has faith in us, we can uplift everyone we meet by saying, "I have confidence in you."

Often as a woman comes up to me after a seminar, I will encourage her to move on in her search for fulfillment, and I tell her "I know you can do it." I may meet her a few years later and she'll come up to me smiling and say, "It was that day you put your hand on my shoulder and said I could do it that changed my life." I know my words can't change a life, but by showing confidence in someone I don't even know, I can give them the possibility for change.

In order for our children to grow up with a mature sense of self-confidence, we must start building them up when they are little. From the time my son Fred was a toddler, I've trained him to do housework. At 2 he could drag a plastic laundry basket from room to room and fill it with dirty clothes. He'd often dump it and refill it, but eventually he would get it all to the laundry room. As soon as he could distinguish between black and white, I'd have him sort the laundry in two piles. Later he understood "delicate wash" from heavy towels. Sorting wash is a positive occupation for the little ones, as it's already dirty and they can't hurt it. As a teen, young Fred did his own laundry, and as I began to travel constantly, he did everyone's laundry. Because he's Melancholy, he not only did the wash but did it perfectly.

By the time he was 20, Fred ran my house and kept the yard in order. When I returned I knew there would be no dirty dishes in the sink, the towels would be folded neatly, and there would be fresh flowers on the table.

Why did he do this? Did he have a spiritual gift for housework? No. It's because over the years I told him I knew he could do these things, and when he did I praised him. When I would leave for a seminar, I'd say, "Fred, I'm going to tell the ladies about you. I'm going to let them know I can count on you."

He wouldn't say a word, but inside he knew. He knows to this day that I'm saying to myself, *"I'm sure* he will do what I ask and even more."

As the Lord has brought a group of outstanding women together for my CLASS staff, I have given each one the confidence that I believe she will do an exceptional job in teaching people. Right from their first day I have helped them find their passion, shown them how to put it all together and then listened as they presented. People in the audience say, "I watch you while the others are speaking, and you listen as if it were the first time you'd ever heard them." Yes, I pay attention to every word. I want each speaker to know "I have confidence in you."

They know I care about every part of their lives. They know I have faith in what they're doing. They know I believe in them.

I'm sure they will always do what I've taught them and even more.

Conclusion

When Paul had a difficult human relations problem to handle, he started with a *compliment,* showed genuine *concern,* and offered *congratulations.* He phrased the conflict in such a way that he gave a *compromise* right in the beginning. He let Philemon make a *choice:* "Because I love you I'll leave the decision up to you." Paul *challenged* him to stretch beyond his natural inclination and to welcome Onesimus back "just as you would welcome me." And then he affirmed Philemon's choice by saying, "I know, I am sure, I have *confidence* in you."

The *conclusion* was that Philemon responded positively to a negative situation. He chose to rise to the challenge and live up to the confidence Paul showed in him. Because of this compromise, Paul and Philemon stayed friends and Onesimus saw true love and forgiveness, which challenged him to full-time Christian service.

What will be your conclusion? Are you *willing* to make the effort it takes to get along with others?

Even with difficult people?

It's not easy to put other people's interests before our own. It's not natural to find their needs and fill them when we're craving to have someone believe in us. We have to decide whether it's worth the effort or whether we just want to have our own way.

We have to ask ourselves:

- How important is it that I make my point, that I win?

- Why do I need the approval of this other person?

- Does it really matter?

From the time I was a child, I remember seeking my mother's approval. I always did well in everything I tackled, and I knew enough not to attempt sports, art, or music because I had no talent in these areas. My mind could learn the rules, principles, or keyboard, but my body wouldn't cooperate. My mother, a violin and cello teacher, was disappointed that I couldn't even hold the bow correctly, so I set out to excel where I could. I got good grades and hoped that Mother would praise me.

Once when I asked her why she didn't tell other people how well I was doing in school, after Peggy's mother had bragged about her, she replied, "You never know when you'll have to eat your words."

Another time she said, "I don't want you to get a swelled head."

Throughout life I've tried to pull a compliment out of Mother, but, while she was never negative, she hung in at neutral. One day in my mother's later years, I went to visit her in Braswell's Retirement Hotel. I'd shown her my exciting schedule of speaking, including a European trip, a Cancun retreat, and an Alaskan cruise. As I waited for her to give me an encouraging word, she looked at the schedule and said, "It's amazing you're so busy considering what you do is something nobody needs."

I was discouraged, and I told Fred of this comment. He looked up and said, "When are you going to grow up and be able to function without your mother's approval?" I was shocked at this question. I was grown up, and my success didn't depend on my mother's approval—or did it?

Fred continued, "How old is your mother?"

"Eighty-five."

"Has she praised you much before?"

"No."

"Then what makes you think in her dying days that she'll get excited over what you're doing now? If she hasn't been enthusiastic about your life before, what makes you expect she'll change now?" As I looked stunned at his analysis, he added, "Why don't you stop trying to get out of your mother what she can't give you and start giving her what she needs."

I wish I could say I enjoyed Fred's analysis and that I was so spiritual that I leaped for his solution.

Instead, I just kept quiet and thought about it. But the more I thought about it, the more I realized he was right. My mother is a Phlegmatic personality, not given to enthusiasm or vain praises. I am part Sanguine, wanting credit and applause for what I do. How childish of me, understanding the different temperaments well, to be seeking for something my mother's nature couldn't give. I was being a difficult person.

As this truth sank into me, I realized a principle in getting along with people: *We should give them what they desire and not be looking for them to fill our needs.* Was I able to do this? Once I faced the situation, I was eager to act upon it.

I asked myself, "What does my mother need in her waning years?" She needs to know that she's important and that she's not been thrown into that large elderly wastebasket. What does my telling her about my trips do for her? It makes her feel older and of little significance. It in no way builds her up. It makes the difference between our lives—mine exciting and adventurous, hers dull and sedentary—even greater. I was approaching her all wrong. I was looking for the mother to praise the little girl when I should have been the daughter seeking to build her aging mother's self-esteem.

As I stopped talking at her and began listening to her, I gained a new respect for her attitude. One day she said, "I guess my life has been hard, but I've never looked at it that way as I was going through it."

I began to pray and ask the Lord, "What does my mother need?" I expected the Lord to give me a grocery list: ice cream, cookies, a geranium. But instead all that came to me was, "Ask your mother how she likes it there." I didn't want to do that because she'd always said to me, "Don't ever put me in one of those places." And I had. But the next time I went over, I asked, "Mom, how do you like it here?" She smiled as she said softly, "This is the best place I've ever lived."

"Why?" I asked in disbelief.

"The very first day when they assigned me my seat, they put me at the head of the table and gave *me* the only chair with arms on it."

What a beautiful summary of my mother's last days. She had finally been put at the head of the table, and she had the only chair with arms on it.

Here I had been trying for years to get her excited over the size of my chair, and all she had wanted was for someone to put her at the head of the table in a chair with arms on it.

I thank the Lord that Fred asked me when I was going to grow up and *stop seeking from my mother what she couldn't give and start giving her what she needed.*

I began to appreciate Mother's Phlegmatic and accepting nature. She didn't get enthused, but she never complained about her circumstances. She was not a difficult person. The next time I was home, I had my mother over for dinner. I realized how I had always seated her on the side of the table, next to the difficult people, because she listened well and could get along with anybody. That night I cooked a meal she liked, a New England boiled dinner. I realized I had often served her experimental dishes thinking it was my job to expand her culinary horizons. I gave her the red plate that said "You're Special," seated her at the head of the table, and gave her my chair, the one with arms on it.

That evening I spent with Mother, as the cancer had brought her from 130 pounds down to 93, she said, "I'm so grateful I don't have any pain. So many of the ladies at the home are in constant pain, and many are crippled and can't walk. I'm comfortable. I'm just tired."

After I went on the road again, Lauren brought her grandmother home to the room in Lauren's house where she had lived for three years before Braswell's. Lauren washed and set her hair, and Mother picked the first rose off her special bush outside her window. She sat in her room and played with her two great-grandsons. That night, back in the retirement home, she called her sister Jean in Massachusetts and said, "I wish it were all over, but I'm feeling fine. I'm just tired." She cut the tags off a new nightgown that my son had given her for Christmas. As with many of her gifts, this gown had been "too good to wear." As if she knew this was a special night, she put the gown on, went to sleep, and never woke up.

At the funeral my two brothers and I gave eulogies of what Mother's sweet and gentle spirit had meant to us, and I was able to say, "All she wanted was to sit at the head of the table and have a chair with arms on it. Now we know that she is seated at the right hand of the Father, and He has surely put her at the head of the table and given her a chair with arms on it."

Ask yourself today, in your human relationships: Are you looking for other people to fill your needs, to give you approval?

If you are, you will never be happy and you might be thought of as a difficult person. To get along with others we have to ask ourselves:

- What is their need?

• How can I fill it?

I had learned to stop seeking from my mother what she couldn't give, and to start giving her what she had always needed: a little honor, a bit of respect, a special chair.

Don't wait until it's too late; I almost did. Find out what those other people need and give it to them. It may be as simple as a seat at the head of the table, a chair with arms on it. When you give to other people looking for nothing in return, they may look at *you* in a whole new light. Don't make your mother, father, husband, or wife wait until they get to heaven to sit at the head of the table. Give them what they need today.

> If you wish to be a success
> And do all that you are able
> Find someone in need of a chair
> And seat them at the head of the table.

Parade of Pious Personalities Skit

Introduction

I first created the *Parade of Pious Personalities* for the Arizona Women's Retreat in 1973. Using only an outline and a list of Bible verses, I ad-libbed what turned out to be a hilarious fashion show caricaturing different types of saintly women. The response was overwhelming, and what started out as a one-night-stand has become a classic and now a book, *How to Get Along with Difficult People.*

If your church group or club wants a humorous skit with a message that takes little preparation and has no lines to memorize, this is it. Select women (or men if you wish to expand the cast) who love to ham it up on stage and have them create their own costumes as suggested.

You can use as few or as many of these characters as you wish, according to the time you have and whether it is a function just for women or the whole church. Even though this started out as a spoof of a fashion show, I have broadened it to be an overview of church characters in hope that people will see themselves or at least see how to get along with those "difficult people"!

Parade of Pious Personalities

To do this as a skit, the setting should be a church sanctuary. The characters should be dressed in extremes of their personalities. It is important that the Narrator have an excellent speaking voice and exceptional diction. He or she must also have a sense of humor and be able to bounce with whatever the characters do. Since the narrator IS the show, this person must be willing to practice the material and not expect to read it at the last minute. The characters should be challenged to react visibly and give the audience something to laugh about. Remind them they are caricatures, exaggerations of real people.

Give each person a copy of their description from the script so they can see how they are described. This will help them create their costumes and get the right props. Each person will come up and cross the stage before going to their places.

At the beginning we see a large chair at one side. This area should imitate, even exaggerate, a glitzy Christian talk show set.

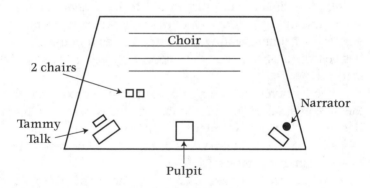

NARRATOR: Today we once again continue our award-winning Christian daytime serial *Parade of Pious Personalities.* Even though we know we are saved, sanctified, and on our way to heaven, the world does not always understand. We hear the music of the Crystal Covenant Choir singing our theme song

"The Little Brown Church in the Vale" as our hostess, Tammy Talk, appears on the set.

TAMMY TALK enters as music from a choir or tape is heard. She should be over-dressed, perhaps have a bouffant wig, throw kisses to the audience, and have available a string of large pearls as the gift of the month.

TAMMY: Thank you, thank you, thank you for tuning in today! Many of you listeners have been with us since we worshiped in the original Little Brown Church in the Vale before we built, with your generous contributions, the Big Brown Church on the Move. You may remember when Past-Pastor Paul Perfect was called to the pulpit and pondered over the pitiful plight of the church plant. You may be one of the thousands who responded to his plea for plentiful provision for God's people. You may be among those who received the snakeskin-covered Bible with your own initials in rhinestones at absolutely no charge when you sent in $10,000 to the building fund. Or you might be one who bought a brick at $500 apiece or paid $1,000 if you wanted your name etched on the brick before you personally plastered it in place as the parishioner who paid for it. So many of you listeners have been faithful to your pledges, so keep those cards and letters coming. Our new financial opportunity for this month will allow you to put a deposit on your own timeshare room, with a view of Mount Rushmore, in the Helen Brown Rice Retirement Residence, named for the daughter of our founder, Little Brown. The first hundred people rushing in their riches will receive a string of priceless pearl prayer beads as a generous gift reminding them to pray for the rest of the payments. Be among the first to secure your spot in the sanctity of this senior citizen city of tomorrow.

As she leaves the stage, the NARRATOR is heard again.

NARRATOR: Remember, in review, how Past-Pastor Paul Perfect produced a powerful church full of precious people, and then, according to the Peter Principle, he was taken from his place of prominence and elevated to the presidency of the Graduate School of Pastoral Profundity. The pulpit committee, tired of Pastor Perfect's sermons on Greek derivatives, searched for a new pastor with personality, and chose Sam Sermon from On-the-Mount Ministries.

The Big Brown Church prides itself on its people: blameless, harmless, and sinless. The bylaws state that no imperfect members will be admitted, although somewhere along the line a few difficult people drifted in.

THE NARRATOR *continues as each person enters, reacts, comes down the aisle, and goes to the place mentioned. The aim here is to characterize the perfect people of the parish so the audience will have fun while analyzing themselves. The costumes are suggestions and you may add or delete items as it fits your group.*

Sally Spiritual

SALLY SPIRITUAL—*needs to be in black, carry Bibles and a sign saying "Repent and Be Saved," and wear a large cross and a funny hat with a lily. She needs a large ring of keys that she rattles. Conversation can be done by the* NARRATOR *or by* SALLY *or* MARVIN.

NARRATOR: While Paul Perfect was pastor, the parish was kept pure, but when Sam Sermon was selected, he didn't seem to care who came to church as long as they contributed. As Sister Sally Spiritual says, "We gave him an inch and he took a mile." Sally always has words of wisdom to share with anyone who'll listen. She's always the first one in on Sunday morning to make sure the sanctuary is set up properly. She's tried to delegate the responsibility, but no one does it right. She personally created the chartreuse altar cloth and embroidered Adam and Eve in gold holding a basket of red apples. Sally is always glad to explain to visitors the symbolism expressed by this creative stitchery: that if we reach for one sin, we may soon have a basketful. Sally is the only one allowed to conduct tours of the church, as the original was built by her grandfather Silas Spiritual in 1902, and her mother, Sadie Spiritual, played the organ from the day it was installed until her untimely death the day after she won the Senior Citizen Scripture Contest at the District Convention.

To begin the *Parade of Pious Personalities* on this Sunday morning, we see Sally arriving early to open up the church. [SALLY *enters from the rear.*] As she always says, "It's the early bird that catches the biggest worms." You will notice that Sally, as usual, is wearing biblical black from head to toe. Her classic Christian hat is adorned by a lowly lily of the field and is modestly veiled. As superintendent of the Sunday school, Sally always carries coordinating black leather Bibles and a concordance for easy reference. Sally's only jewelry is a large cross, immediately identifying her as a believing Christian to the heathen world.

Sally has been a Christian for as long as she can remember. Right from her childhood, Sally was spiritual. She never desired any worldly possessions and never was tempted by the lusts of the flesh. Sally never smoked or drank; she never swore or gossiped; she never played cards or sewed on Sunday. Frankly, Sally is often shocked by the sins of others, and she prays for many fallen friends, plus a few heathen in China.

Sally knows all the spiritual greats of the century, and she loves to tell how her mother once dated Billy Graham's cousin and how her grandfather once bought shoes from D.L. Moody. It brings tears to her eyes to realize she was in the same elevator with Emilie Barnes at the Sunday School convention but was too stunned to get her autograph.

Sally spends much of her time in church, for, as she always says, "When the cat's away, the mice will play." On Monday nights she attends the pastor's Bible study on "The Deeper Pleasures of Personal Piety." On Tuesday nights she goes to the Missionary Society, where she is president of the Prudish Priscilla Circle. On Wednesday nights she rushes over to the prayer meeting, where the current topic is "Is Heaven for the Hindu?" On Thursdays she has to go early to pass out the books at choir rehearsal, where director Marvin Music is putting spiritual words to the *Phantom of the Opera* to create a clever cantata for Christmas. On Fridays Sally has to bring a casserole to the Pioneer Girls' Potluck Supper and Sing-Along, and on Saturday nights she has to chaperone the Teen Taco Treat and Hayride.

Today is Sunday, her busiest day of the whole week. She rises early to bake cookies for the coffee break. Since Sally is the only one with a complete set of keys to every door and cupboard, she must be "Johnny-on-the-spot." See her clanking ring of keys, which she has already used to open up the high-arched front door, hand-carved by her Uncle Creative. She now must check the chairs for junior church and then unlock the closet for the choir robes.

Some people have suggested that Sally should not have so much responsibility, but she always says, "If you can't count on the granddaughter of the man who built the church, whom can you ever count on?"

Sally's life is dedicated to the church, and she can recite the whole book of Philemon, but some people find her difficult.

Marvin Music

MARVIN MUSIC—*As* MARVIN *enters he calls "Sally." He is dressed perfectly; looks with disdain on* SALLY, *and disgust on* SAM. *He carries music, pens, baton and laser light and busies himself in the choir loft. When ready he sits down on the front row of the choir and works on his music.*

NARRATOR: Sally jumps as she hears her name called in the empty church. It is Marvin Music, who needs the keys to the organ and choir cabinet. As Sally hands him two large keys, she reminds Marvin, "It was my mother who played this organ brilliantly for 47 years until her untimely death..."

"Yes, I've heard." Marvin has no time for trivia, and he finds Sally especially offensive.

He always seems preoccupied, Sally muses, but he sure does dress well. [Sally *exits, jingling her keys. She reenters the choir loft when the* G-Clef girls *come on.*] Indeed, Marvin is a perfectionist. His pin-striped three-piece suit is a classic, his white shirt is so starched it could stand without him, and his tie is adorned with notes forming the first line of "The Old Rugged Cross." Marvin always carries the sheet music for the choir because "you can't trust anyone else."

Marvin checks his pockets. He has his three black pens: fine tip, medium tip, and felt tip. He has his collapsible baton and pointer, and his penlight in case he ever has to conduct in the dark. Marvin is prepared for any possible disaster and always expects the worst. He has his music planned out from now through Christmas and feels if anything's worth doing, it's worth doing right.

Sam Sermon

Sam Sermon—*Looks thrown together and exhausted. He needs to carry a shabby briefcase. Change his description to whatever he wears.* SAM *goes to the pulpit, where he drops his briefcase. As* SAM *gathers his papers and stuffs them back in his briefcase,* JOYCE *appears.* SAM *sits in the pulpit chair meditating on his sermon.*

NARRATOR: Here comes Pastor Sam Sermon. Marvin can't stand Sam because he's so sloppy and keeps changing his mind about the order of the service and expects Marvin to be flexible. Artistic people need to think and plan ahead. They shouldn't be expected to change at the last minute what they've practiced all week. Marvin is always right, but some people find him difficult. Marvin retreats to the choir loft so he won't have to talk to Sam.

Sam Sermon bounces up to the platform, singing off-key, totally oblivious to Marvin cringing in the choir loft. Sam always comes on too strong for Marvin, and he never seems to have his act together. He ran out of gas this morning and had to walk from the corner. As he hunts for his sermon notes in his overstuffed briefcase, he throws everything out on the platform until he finds the McDonald's napkin where he had jotted down his thoughts while out for an Egg McMuffin with his two-year-old son. Sam doesn't believe in detailed notes—they only confuse you—and half the fun of preaching is making it up while you're on your feet. You never go stale that way.

Sam's hair is sticking out like a briar bush from his walk in the wind, and his green tie is crooked, but who will be able to take their eyes off his red, black, and white plaid sport coat long enough to notice? Sam was brought up in a church where the pastor wore a black robe, and he vowed if *he* ever had a congregation of his own he'd wear bright clothes to cheer up the parishioners.

Just looking at Sam depresses Marvin, who clears his throat and sings his scales. Sam jumps, knocking his glass of water onto his napkin of notes. "Now you've ruined my sermon," he cries out.

"It won't be the first time your sermon's been ruined," Marvin muses.

Marvin wonders if Sam will ever grow up. He was voted most likely to succeed in college, but he's never lived up to his potential. Sam's never had a knack for numbers, and he feels that balancing a checkbook is a waste of time. "It's either there or it isn't," he chuckles. Usually it isn't. Sam is frequently short of money, and he goes to the men's room when it's time for the waitress to bring the check. "God loves a cheerful giver," he reminds his friends. Sam still doesn't understand why the finance chairman quit when he found Sam had taken money from the World Hunger Fund to entertain his children at the San Diego Zoo. Marvin thinks to himself, "Sam's sermons are funny, but they seldom have a clear point, and he often runs overtime. When he goes too long, he just tells me to cut the music." Sam loves people and hugs everyone on his way to the pulpit chair, but he can never remember their names. Sam shrugs, "What difference does it make? I just call them all 'honey' and they love me."

And most of them do, but some people such as Marvin find Sam difficult.

JOYCE JUDGING—*Needs a "Moses tablet" that says "Thou Shalt Not" and pure white clothes. She flirts with* MARVIN *as she heads to the organ. She has a yardstick to measure sins, which she does as she comes down the aisle. She settles in by the organ and occasionally winks and waves at* MARVIN.

NARRATOR: Most vocal in criticizing the pastor and parishioners is Joyce Judging, who comes from a long line of people with discerning spirits. As far as Joyce is concerned, the Christian

Joyce Judging

life is a long list of don'ts for other people, and she feels that God has appointed her as the watchdog of the community. Joyce has a great memory for biblical instruction, and she feels led to tell other people where they are wrong and how they could improve to be like her. She loves to teach on the gifts of the Spirit and to show how she was personally anointed by the Lord Himself with the gifts of correction and direction.

She loves to tell how the Lord Himself led her down a dim alley to a pawn shop in Tel Aviv, where she found the original marble tablet of Moses saying "Thou shalt not." During the week she keeps it on her mantel at home as a warning to her children, lest they stray from the straight and narrow, but on Sundays she carries it with her as a sign of obedience.

This morning (as usual) Joyce is wearing pristine white to emphasize her purity. Joyce often shares at prayer meeting that her husband is not really a Christian, and she has pointed out to the children, "Daddy is not one of us!" Joyce knows so much more about God's laws than her husband that she feels called to point out his faults. She tells him constantly what a miserable sinner he is. She won't ever let him relax in his own home, and she nags him daily about his personal habits that hinder his hope for heaven. All their marriage problems are his fault, and she knows she could someday be happy if only he would shape up.

Joyce plays the organ on Sunday morning because it gives her the best vantage point from which to view the audience. Those she can't see over her left shoulder she can pick up in the mirror. "It's amazing what people will do when they don't think anyone is looking," Joyce confides to Marvin. Joyce confides a lot to Marvin. In fact, she sits next to him as often as possible. Since her husband isn't well, Joyce believes it's always good to have a Plan B firmly in mind, just in case.

Joyce Judging is always open to learning new truths, and this very afternoon she, Marvin Music, and the entire choir will be attending the new symposium "Music in Your Mid-Life Crisis." Joyce has taken courses on the "Inner Life," the "Outer Life," and the "Upper Life." She has been baptized, sanctified, catechized, confirmized, and mesmerized, but all that her religious training seems to have done is provide her with a larger yardstick by which to measure the sins of other people.

Joyce is sincere, studious, and sinless—on the surface—but there are some people who find her superiority difficult.

Bob Bossy—Dr. Bossy *is a wealthy businessman with a beeper he can set off. He carries ledgers, charts, and moneybags. He sits by* Sam *and shows him the ledgers.*

Narrator: It's now 10:45, and Dr. Bob Bossy drives up to the front door in his Mercedes and parks at the foot of the steps, blocking the sidewalk. He feels the "No Parking" sign is to keep other people out of his spot. Everyone knows he's the

Bob Bossy

busiest doctor in town and must have his car available in case of emergencies. You'll notice he has the church ledgers in his arms so he can give a report to Sam Sermon before the service. He has his beeper on his belt to buzz him if a baby should want to be born between "Brighten the Corner" and the benediction. No one knows he can activate the beeper by himself, so if church goes overtime or he's in a dull meeting, he taps the unit and off it goes. Why, there it goes now!

People are in awe of Dr. Bossy's busy lifestyle and the money bags he carries for the week's deposits, and Sam Sermon is impressed with his position and prestige. With just one call to the bank he was able to get a loan large enough to build a basketball court out of the ladies' parlor and mount a new steeple higher than the one on the Baptist Church across the street. Sam appointed Bob chairman of the Board of Elders, and Bob's first move was to make a large chart—which he carries with him—delineating everyone's area of control. Some who had been on the board for years were shocked to find they had responsibilities. "It's about time this place was run as a business," Bob stated at the annual meeting. "Until we get the budget balanced we're going to cut out air conditioning and charge for communion."

Bob Bossy is busy balancing the budget and controlling Sam but has little time for his family or friends. In spite of his money, some people find Dr. Bossy difficult.

Debbie Depressed

DEBBIE DEPRESSED—*Needs an old robe, fuzzy slippers, and pink rollers. She carries a bag of cookies, a droopy stuffed dog, and a huge bottle labeled "pills." She moves slowly up the aisle, comes up on the platform to pour out her troubles to* SAM, *and when appropriate, heads for the choir room. She appears later with a choir robe over her outfit and her curlers removed.*

NARRATOR: As we watch, Dr. Bossy lays down his moneybags and reviews the ledgers with Sam, Joyce Judging mulls over her music at the organ, Marvin Music agonizes over his anthems, Sally Spiritual rearranges her Bibles, and Sam Sermon desperately tries to reconstruct his sermon notes. The noise we hear is Debbie Depressed driving up in her old Dodge with the dents. Oh my, she's really depressed this morning as she didn't bother to get dressed. The last time she came to church in her bathrobe with those fuzzy old slippers, Marvin Music was furious. But she pointed out that the choir robe covers her up so what difference does it make how she looks? She leaves her pink rollers in until it's time to march in so the curl will last through lunch. She has a bag of cookies with her in case her blood sugar drops, and you'll notice that even her stuffed dog looks depressed. Her own personal black cloud hovers over her as she walks up the aisle to the choir loft. She's really too tired to sing, but she's afraid if she stays home people will talk about her—and they probably would. Debbie finds it difficult to make decisions, and when friends ask her out, she has to pray about it for weeks. Her favorite verse is Job 10:1 TLB: "I am weary of living." Debbie gets depressed over every little thing. She's weighed down with her weight, but she's too weary to exercise and hopes to drown her pounds in milk shakes. Nothing ever goes right for Debbie. She's the black sheep of the family. Her father wanted a boy, and her mother has never liked her.

The thought of housework overwhelms her. She gets discouraged over baskets of wrinkled laundry, but she can't bring herself to iron. One day she forced herself to clean the whole house, but no one noticed, so she quit. Much of the time Debbie pulls down the shades and won't answer the phone. She weeps in loneliness, but she really doesn't like people. She is a full-time counsel-seeker and details her depression to anyone who'll listen. Just last week when Evangelist Billy Braggart had a revival, Debbie rededicated her life each night, but she never seemed to improve.

Debbie is frequently ill, but the doctors can't find anything wrong. Her husband says it's all in her head, and she sighs, "No one really knows what I go through." Debbie has pills to pep her up and pills to calm her down. She takes them all to balance out her day. Each afternoon she watches the soaps and hopes someday to be healed by *General Hospital*. She always needs the pastor's counsel, and just yesterday she said to him, "I might as well just end it all, but I'm afraid no one would come to the funeral."

Sam feels sorry for Debbie, but some people find her difficult.

Harriet Hurry

HARRIET HURRY—*Wears a jogging suit with a large clock face hanging around her neck and several watches on her wrist. She has calendars and planners she checks as she jogs the aisles, crosses the platform, greets everyone she sees, and exits to the nursery.*

NARRATOR: As Debbie settles down to pour out her problems to Sam we see Harriet Hurry running down the aisle in her Christian Dior jogging suit and matching Nike shoes. Since Harriet is always in a hurry, she wears a large clock so she can keep track of the time while on the run, and several watches set to the times of the major capitals of the world. Harriet is an extremely competent lady, and no one knows how she finds the time to be the coordinator of Manna on

Wheels, director of Hemming for Heathens, on the board of the Current Crucial Crises Council, and president of the Spiritual Jogging Society. She often rushes into a meeting late, gives a dramatic report, and leaves early to make it to the next meeting. Harriet's theme song is "I'm late, I'm late, for a very important date."

Harriet is out to save the world, and her husband calls her "The Lone Arranger." Harriet spends every Monday morning coordinating her calendars, and she has to check each day's schedule carefully. If you were to ask her out for lunch, she would not have a free day until the year 2050.

Harriet thrives on activity. If she can't find some, she'll create some. She is constantly moving furniture, redecorating the living room, or pouring a cement patio on the backyard. Harriet feels her friends and family are all lazy, and she is always trying to whip them into shape. She keeps a timer with her so she can check her children at their chores and constantly press them into improving their efficiency.

Harriet is too busy to be a real friend or to think a deep thought. Someday she'll have time for Bible study. Someday she'll have time for her children. Someday she'll have time for cooking. Until then, the family will have to get along on Big Macs and Lean Cuisine. Harriet may look a little casual for Sunday, but she only runs the nursery, and what do those babies care about her outfit?

Harriet can get more done in a shorter time than anyone in church, but some people find her difficult.

MARTHA MARTYR—*Looks humble and worn out carrying mops, pails, and a tray of communion cups. She polishes and dusts the pews and the audience as she comes in looking ever so burdened. She may have someone hold the tray of cups when she needs to*

Martha Martyr

*polish harder. When she is done she should fall into a front pew and
go to sleep.*

NARRATOR: Here comes Martha Martyr bringing out the trays of
communion cups. It's her job to keep them clean, and she
takes her duties very seriously. On Sundays Martha wears a
conservative high-necked dress, lest she cause the church
men to lust in their hearts. Martha never wears makeup, lest
she appear worldly, and never a smile, lest she seem frivolous.
Martha considers the Christian life to be one of extreme self-
sacrifice and service to others. She always carries coordinating mops, pails, cloths, and cleaners to church in order to
polish the communion table and pulpit. While Martha is not
concerned with the latest fashions, she is always scrupulously
clean and prepared for the daily duties that drop upon her.

Martha is always willing to stop scrubbing long enough to
tell you about the time she washed all the diapers for the
pastor's new baby even though she had a migraine headache.

She is the only deaconess who will scrub the church basement floor, and she does the dishes at each church supper

after all the others have gone home and abandoned her. You can be sure that when Martha has done the dishes you will be able to see your face reflected in each plate.

Martha entertains all the visiting missionaries who pass through town because no one else really wants them. She feeds them simple food so they won't get spoiled before going back to the mission field. She collects old clothes for the missionaries (who, frankly, dress better than Martha).

Martha is a fanatical housekeeper, and she is constantly picking lint off furniture and friends, and especially Sam Sermon, who never looks quite put together. She rushes to fluff up the pillows the minute a person gets up from her couch, and she straightens pictures in everybody's home. Martha cooks constantly, and she recently preserved 40 jars of her specialty, "Mustard Seed and Okra." Her children are all fat, and she makes them sit at the table until they have stuffed down every last bite. If one child dares to object, Martha gives a mournful tale about all the poor, starving children in China. Martha constantly hovers over her husband, hands him his fork, cuts up his meat, and tells him of all her friends who don't really care for their men. Martha bleaches her husband's underwear, mends all his socks, and even presses his permanent-press shirts. Martha tells everyone how hard she works and what a noble mother she really is. Frankly, Martha is weary in well-doing and sighs a lot, but underneath she is so eager for the credit that she would rather die dusting than train a child to work.

Martha does every job at church that no one else will do and then tells Sam Sermon about it so he will praise her from the pulpit. Martha has an endless need for affirmation, especially from people of prestige. Martha's life seems full of ups and downs. One moment she's weighed down with the cares of the world, and the next she's giving a dramatic presentation of some personal problem in her past. Martha hides nothing from her friends, who have heard endless stories of her deprived childhood. She has told them so often of her years of malnutrition that they feel guilty when they eat. She always has the church ladies in tears on testimony night when she tells of how her drunken father ran off with the town floozy, leaving her consumptive mother with the 11 children, just the day before the tornado took the house.

Martha is overworked, overwrought, and overdone, and she slumps down to rest quite often. The church doesn't know what it would do without Martha Martyr, but some people find her difficult.

Larry Lazy

Larry Lazy—*He should be casually handsome and hug a few of the audience ladies. He should go up and greet* Sam *before heading to the back door to pass out a handful of bulletins.*

Narrator: It's almost time for church to start, and Larry Lazy isn't here yet to pass out the bulletins. Larry never likes to get involved in church activities, but he can always see how other people could have done it better. He did agree to come once a month and be an usher because it seemed about the easiest thing to do (and one should help out one's local church). Larry never gets enthused about any of the programs, and when he heard they were planning a workday for all men to put up the steeple, he threatened to leave the church if he was required to come.

Larry's a pleasant fellow—in fact here he is now, ambling up the front steps in his cords and a sweater. He's passing out the bulletins and smiling at all the ladies, who find his cool, laid-back look appealing.

His wife, however, shared at Women's Confession Circle last week that she couldn't get him off the couch since he got the remote control for the TV. Their grass is up to the windowsills, and the outside ivy is crawling in through the cracks in the windows. Larry says he's waiting until they come out with robot lawnmowers, and he feels the invading ivy is attractive and saves on watering houseplants. Last week a piece of the roof fell in over the baby's bed, but he told his wife to pretend it was a skylight. It drives his wife crazy that he makes light of serious problems, but the other women think he's adorable.

Everybody loves Larry Lazy, but some people who have to rely on him find him difficult.

WINNIE WITNESS—*A female evangelist in loud clothes. She should have a red T-shirt with "Expect a Miracle" or something similar. She also needs a basket of tracts and wears a "Good News Glove" (available through Campus Crusade for Christ if not in your local Bible bookstore). She goes up to hug* SAM *and reacts to the* NARRATOR. *She starts to leave and then sees* JOE JOCK. *She drops her baskets and runs to him. After they parade around together, they settle down in a back pew.*

Winnie Witness

NARRATOR: Here comes Winnie Witness on her way to teach her second-grade Sunday school class. She's full of pep and energy and always wears a skirt of many colors and her red T-shirt, which reads "Expect a Miracle." Winnie looks perpetually for potential converts and smiles all the time so people will ask how they can be happy like her.

Notice that Winnie is carrying a complimentary straw basket filled with hundreds of different evangelistic tracts. She has the plan of salvation in 12 languages and is willing to witness to the uttermost parts of the world.

To accent her stunning outfit, Winnie is wearing a pair of plastic Good News Gloves. By having her gloves on, she is always ready to explain God's plan in living color to any little lost child who doesn't know Jesus. Each finger on the glove is a different color: Green is the lost child, yellow is God's love, black is for sin, red is Christ's death, and white says, "I receive Him."

You would never guess that Winnie is a new Christian. She's the chairperson of the Church Evangelism Committee even though she just became a believer at last spring's retreat at Pinkney Pines. When she came down the hill bursting with her new faith, she drove right over to her mother-in-law's home and told her that she was a sinner not yet saved by grace, that she attended a shallow church, and that she'd better leave her liberal denomination immediately.

Winnie then informed her husband that she would no longer go to the church of his youth because she didn't even think the pastor was a Christian. She immediately shared her faith with her husband, using the newest witnessing booklet. When he wouldn't pray with her, she told him he was hopeless, and she would shake the dust off her feet and go.

Today, as every day, Winnie was up early and out of the house seeking the lost. Her beds are unmade, and the dishes are in the sink, but she is witnessing aggressively to everyone she meets. Winnie grabs people wherever she finds them, backs them against the wall, and asks, with a persuasive smile, "Is there any reason you would not want to become a Christian my way, now?" She turns everything into a time of testimony, and when her friends see her coming, they flee in the opposite direction. Winnie is determined to bring her husband into the kingdom, so she tapes verses to his mirror, puts big Bibles under his pillow, and hides tracts in his lunch pail. She must get to her Sunday school class, so she bustles off, giving a big smile and a wave to those already in the pews.

Winnie got an A in assertion training, but some people find her difficult.

JOE JOCK—*Must be tall, handsome, athletic, and not embarrassed to parade around in his gym clothes and flex his muscles.*

Joe Jock

Narrator: Winnie turns to see one of her new converts coming to church for the first time. Joe Jock is 6 feet 6 inches tall. He's arrived at the Big Brown Church in his gym clothes. Winnie wants to show him off, so she walks him down the aisle while smiling at everyone. Joe is strikingly handsome, like a Greek god. Winnie tells him so, and he whispers that he's modeled for art classes, been the inspiration for the marble statue of Alexander the Great on the town green, and been on many TV shampoo and cologne commercials.

Wow!

Joe's whole interest in life is his body and sports. As a boy he used the crib as a trampoline and lifted rattles to develop his muscles. In grammar school he was captain of every team, and in high school he earned every letter and sweater available. He won an athletic scholarship to Anxious State, where he majored in physical education. Each morning he was up at 5:30 working out with weights before going to his classes in Prevention of Muscular Atrophy and Inclement Weather Activities. For Joe an exciting date is going to college track meets, hosting tailgate picnics at the Auburn-Ole Miss football game, or watching videos of old Mike Tyson fights.

Now he has marked off the grass in his front yard and has coached his children and the neighborhood kids to play soccer. He is charging the parents to watch.

Winnie remembers how she met Joe at the gym, where she'd gone to evangelize the ladies who had weight problems. He'd been leading the group and noticed her exercising in her Good News Gloves. When he asked her what her button meant that said "WWJD," she said it stood for "What would Jesus do?" He responded, and Winnie led him to the Lord. That day when Winnie met him in the gym, Joe was ready for a new life. His wife had walked out on him—Joe Jock, a hero! She'd told him she was sick of life being a series of World Series. She was no longer willing to be awash with the Lakers, depressed with the Dodgers, or anguished over the Angels. She didn't care if McGwire ever hit another home run or if Michael Jordan would come out of retirement one more time. She'd had it.

So here's Joe in church. He can't believe it himself. Every girl has been crazy about him, but his ex-wife finds him difficult. [JOE *leaves with* WINNIE.]

GLORIA, GILDA, AND GERTRUDE, THE G-CLEF GIRLS—*Enter wearing choir robes.* SALLY *enters choir loft too.*

GLORIA GOSSIP—*Bright and chatty looking, she carries a steno pad and handful of pencils with erasers.*

GILDA GUILT—*Carries her new book, clearly titled* Gilda's Guide to Guilt *in large print.*

GERTRUDE GRUDGE—*Carries her big black book, clearly labeled* Record of Wrongs.

Gloria Gossip   **Gilda Guilt**   **Gertrude Grudge**

The G-Clef Girls

GLORIA *and* GILDA *stand next to* GERTRUDE *and react to her* Record of Wrongs. *When their script is over, they can sing a brief hymn if they wish and ultimately sit in the choir loft.*

NARRATOR: The choir is now gathering for its entrance, dressed in new red robes bought with money raised from the sale of bumper stickers that say: "Get in the Groove, Join the Church on the Move." The trio performing this morning is the "G-Clef Girls" with Gloria Gossip, Gilda Guilt, and Gertrude Grudge. Here comes Gloria now. Gloria considers herself the historian of the church, and she carries a steno pad with her to jot down any new fact or fable. In fact, many of the favorite fables of the church would never have been passed down if it hadn't been for Gloria Gossip. She loves to both listen and talk and always makes her tales so tantalizing that people ask for more. She has a pillow on her couch that reads, "If you have nothing good to say about anyone, sit next to me."

Gloria has never let the truth stand in the way of a good story, and she believes if you tell her a dull tale, it is only right that she improve it enough so the next person won't be as bored with it as she was hearing it from you.

Gloria always writes in pencil so she can erase the facts if she comes up with a better ending to a tragic story. She prints up the secret prayer requests to pass out to all those who have the gift of intercession.

Gloria has trained herself to hear a different conversation with each ear while moving another one out of her mouth. It took years of practice to develop her three-track talent, and she's proud of her ability. She coordinates the church activities and sends out the monthly newsletter full of creative and colorful capers of the church family. Gloria mingles fact with fiction and makes the whole thing fun.

People look forward to her prayer requests and love to read her latest letter, but those who have been hurt by her gossip find her difficult.

Gilda Guilt has her own quiet ministry: manipulation by guilt. She always says, "If you can make people feel guilty, you'll have them under control." When she and her friends go shopping or to meetings, Gilda always drives because the one with the car can always call the shots and be in charge. She teaches guilt classes at guild meetings and shows people how to subtly seize the steering wheel of life.

Gilda carries her new book, *Gilda's Guide to Guilt,* which lists pages of manipulative phrases such as these:

To make grandmothers visit more say:

> "The poor little children hardly remember what you look like. But it's all right, since their other grandmother is here so often."

To slow down people in a hurry say:

"I thought you'd at least have time to look at my new bathroom wallpaper."

To get someone else to have Christmas say:

"I guess I'd better start my Christmas preparations early because I always seem to get stuck with making the dinner and it ruins my whole day."

To keep people visiting longer say:

"Leave now? Why, you just sat down."

To get people to come who've already said no say:

"It's too bad you can't come; I was going to give you a present."

To adult children who won't visit say:

"It's a shame you can't come. I guess I'll have to make out my new will by myself."

Gilda is proud of her book full of comments about local people. "Once you have a book published," Gilda says, "you become an authority and people have to listen to you."

This week Gilda has a church contest in Gloria's newsletter for the best new idea in instilling guilt. She plans to write the most quotable sayings on squares of cloth in liquid embroidery and sew them together into a Guilt Quilt to be auctioned off at the Mother–Daughter Banquet. Gilda often quotes the book *How to Be a Jewish Mother* where it says you must instill guilt in your children so they'll support you in your old age.

The church applauds her creativity, but those who have been manipulated once too often find Gilda difficult.

The third member of the "G-Clef Girls" is Gertrude Grudge. Remember when Gertrude first came to church carrying that huge black book and we all thought it was an oversized large-print Bible? We could tell it was covered in Moroccan leather, but it took Gloria Gossip only a few minutes to inch over and read the gold embossed letters *Record of Wrongs*. Gertrude carries this book for more than its looks, as it contains the names of every single person who has ever wronged her. Gertrude has a brilliant and retentive mind, and her motto is "Never forgive and never forget." To make sure her facts are accurate, she jots down each problem as it occurs, and she has a special section for those people whom even the Lord Himself wouldn't forgive. Gertrude started her book at the age of five as only a precocious child could do. Her first entry was recorded in big print and quotes Aunt Violet, whom she overheard saying, "Poor Gertrude is a homely girl. I do hope she grows out of it."

She remembers how her first-grade teacher would not let her write on the board in colored chalk, and how disappointed she was when she tried out for the role of the rose in the Flower Festival and Miss Dimlick cast her as the thistle. Gertrude remembers how in high school she tried out for cheerleading and the coach put her on the football team. Gertrude has recorded every time she heard her mother-in-law say, "I can't imagine what he ever saw in her in the first place." She has down the name of the nurse who brought in her first baby and said, "They're all ugly in the beginning."

Gertrude knows how many Saturdays her husband watched football when she wanted him to clean the garage, and she has pages of dates when he came home late for dinner. She has many notes on how ungrateful her children are, even after she's stuffed their lunch boxes with Twinkies and softened their shirts with Downy.

Before coming to the Big Brown Church on the Move, Gertrude was the communion cloth chairman of St. Agony's parish. The pastor never did learn her name, and he called her Gertrude Fudge. The choir director would not let her sing a solo on Easter Sunday, the Christian education pastor left her name off the program as the prompter for the Christmas pageant, and the youth leader forbade her from coming to the teen campfire, even after she had donated the marshmallows. So poor Gertrude had no choice but to change churches. Gertrude keeps her *Record of Wrongs* with her at all times lest she forget or be tempted to forgive. Life has been difficult and thankless for Gertrude, but she just grins and records, knowing that at the great day of judgment she will jump up first with the biggest list.

The church admires her memory, but those whose names are in the book consider Gertrude to be difficult.

How great it is that Gloria, Gilda, and Gertrude found each other and now provide harmony for all the difficult people in this perfect church.

As the trio sings a quick Christian song the cast sits quietly. Each one should come to the platform when called and stand there until the end. Each character approaches as the NARRATOR *reads their poem.*

NARRATOR:

Sam Sermon, we all love you
For you are lots of fun,
But we're tired of picking up pieces
Because your work's not done.
So grow up and be responsible,
Slow down and think your life through.
Practice what you preach to us
So your sermons will ring true.

Marvin, you have much talent.
You can compose, direct, and sing.
You always dress so perfectly
And have the bearing of a king,
But when people come to rehearsal
Don't make life seem so dire.
Direct with new excitement
And you'll have a joyful choir.

Dear precious Sally Spiritual,
All dressed in black each day,
Giving out Bible verses
To the sinners you meet on your way.
We applaud your dedication,
Your aim to work and to please.
But could we make a suggestion?
Give somebody else the keys.

Dear Joyce, we're glad to have you
And your yardstick to measure sin.
Your ability to judge all others,
And know those who'll perish or win.
But you've put yourself on a pedestal
With a tablet that says, "thou shalt not"
But if you don't come down with the rest of us,
You won't have a friend in the lot.

"Is there a doctor in the house?"
Is a question we often ask.
But we have our own Bob Bossy
Who is always up to the task.
We know you when your beeper goes off,
We thank you for the new steeple,
But we'd like you a whole lot better
If you were nice to the common people.

Here is our pitiful Debbie,
So sad, always down and depressed.
Do you think you'd feel any better
If you got up each day and got dressed?
If you stopped reviewing all your pains
Remained positive and alert?
So change your habit patterns...
Try smiling. I know it won't hurt.

Harriet, don't you get tired
Running around day and night
Being president of everything
'Cause the others don't do it right?
Try staying home more often,
Stop stirring up turmoil and flurry,
Slow down and let your family know
You're no longer in a hurry.

Martha Martyr, how hard you work
Dusting and mopping all day,
Washing up the communion cups
And putting them all away.
But you turn positives into insults
Then try to find out who said it.
Start helping others as unto the Lord,
And stop looking for worldly credit.

Larry Lazy, you look so handsome
In your cords and yellow sweater.
How could any wife in town
Wish for anyone who's better.
But yours says you won't do a thing,
You're lazy beyond all doubt.
So go home and start to be helpful
Before she throws you out!

Oh Winnie, how every church would love
to have a witnessing angel like you
Who shares her faith with others
Whether hundreds or just a few.
But some people get offended
When you come on too strong.
Stop grabbing each adult or frightened child
For too much *right* makes a *wrong*.

Joe Jock, you've sure got the muscles,
Your abs and your pecs are just fine,
Your knowledge of sports is exceptional,
But your family's been left behind.
So now that you're a new Christian
It's time to go back to your wife.
You'll have enough love to start anew
Now that Jesus is in your life.

Adorable Gloria Gossip,
You don't seem to stick to the facts.
You judge all your cute stories
By how well the person reacts.
It's time you got closer to the truth
And stopped dishing out local dirt.
So edit all your prayer requests
Make sure that no one gets hurt.

Gilda, how bright you seem to be
And what a ministry you've built,
Teaching classes all over the world
On how to manipulate through guilt.
You've been successful in your work,
But you've left victims in your wake,
So let the Lord direct your path.
Be loving for Jesus' sake.

You're carrying your *Record of Wrongs*
And you are Gertrude Grudge,
Who won't forgive a person
Who will not even budge.
But Jesus tells us to forgive,
Seventy times seven,
So throw away your record book,
And we'll see you up in heaven.

TAMMY *appears to conclude the program.*

TAMMY:

Wasn't that touching?
It's caused me to think
I might have some faults
that could cause me to sink.

I'm a little bit like Winnie
Who always is too loud,
And I'm a bit like Harriet
Running from crowd to crowd.

Now that you have seen our show,
Were you reminded of a friend?
Or perhaps your mother-in-law
Who chatters to no end.

Or did you see one like yourself?
Are you Debby, or Sally, or Joyce?
Are you bossy, judgmental, or lazy?
Then it's time to make a choice.

Let's decide to change our ways,
To throw off our negative traits,
To amplify our positives,
And lay aside all weights.

So thanks to our talented cast
For showing us what's right.
We thank you all for coming,
And now to all a good night.

This skit has proven to be both fun and instructive over the years. You have permission to use it in whatever way would be appropriate for your group. You may add to it or delete. You may use all the characters or as few as you wish. You may write in new ones if you have a particular need. If you print up a program, indicate that the narration is from *How to Get Along with Difficult People* by Florence Littauer (Harvest House Publishers).

PERSONALITY PROFILE

Name

DIRECTIONS—In each of the following rows of four words across, place an X in front of one word that most often applies to you. Continue through all forty lines. Be sure each number is marked.

STRENGTHS

1 ___ Animated	___ Adventurous	___ Analytical	___ Adaptable
2 ___ Persistent	___ Playful	___ Persuasive	___ Peaceful
3 ___ Submissive	___ Self-sacrificing	___ Sociable	___ Strong-willed
4 ___ Considerate	___ Controlled	___ Competitive	___ Convincing
5 ___ Refreshing	___ Respectful	___ Reserved	___ Resourceful
6 ___ Satisfied	___ Sensitive	___ Self-reliant	___ Spirited
7 ___ Planner	___ Patient	___ Positive	___ Promoter
8 ___ Sure	___ Spontaneous	___ Scheduled	___ Shy
9 ___ Orderly	___ Obliging	___ Outspoken	___ Optimistic
10 ___ Friendly	___ Faithful	___ Funny	___ Forceful
11 ___ Daring	___ Delightful	___ Diplomatic	___ Detailed
12 ___ Cheerful	___ Consistent	___ Cultured	___ Confident
13 ___ Idealistic	___ Independent	___ Inoffensive	___ Inspiring
14 ___ Demonstrative	___ Decisive	___ Dry humor	___ Deep
15 ___ Mediator	___ Musical	___ Mover	___ Mixes easily
16 ___ Thoughtful	___ Tenacious	___ Talker	___ Tolerant
17 ___ Listener	___ Loyal	___ Leader	___ Lively
18 ___ Contented	___ Chief	___ Chartmaker	___ Cute
19 ___ Perfectionist	___ Permissive	___ Productive	___ Popular
20 ___ Bouncy	___ Bold	___ Behaved	___ Balanced

WEAKNESSES

21 ___ Brassy	___ Bossy	___ Bashful	___ Blank
22 ___ Undisciplined	___ Unsympathetic	___ Unenthusiastic	___ Unforgiving
23 ___ Reluctant	___ Resentful	___ Resistant	___ Repetitious
24 ___ Fussy	___ Fearful	___ Forgetful	___ Frank
25 ___ Impatient	___ Insecure	___ Indecisive	___ Interrupts
26 ___ Unpopular	___ Uninvolved	___ Unpredictable	___ Unaffectionate
27 ___ Headstrong	___ Haphazard	___ Hard to please	___ Hesitant
28 ___ Plain	___ Pessimistic	___ Proud	___ Permissive
29 ___ Angered easily	___ Aimless	___ Argumentative	___ Alienated
30 ___ Naïve	___ Negative attitude	___ Nervy	___ Nonchalant
31 ___ Worrier	___ Withdrawn	___ Workaholic	___ Wants credit
32 ___ Too sensitive	___ Tactless	___ Timid	___ Talkative
33 ___ Doubtful	___ Disorganized	___ Domineering	___ Depressed
34 ___ Inconsistent	___ Introvert	___ Intolerant	___ Indifferent
35 ___ Messy	___ Moody	___ Mumbles	___ Manipulative
36 ___ Slow	___ Stubborn	___ Show-off	___ Skeptical
37 ___ Loner	___ Lord over	___ Lazy	___ Loud
38 ___ Sluggish	___ Suspicious	___ Short-tempered	___ Scatterbrained
39 ___ Revengeful	___ Restless	___ Reluctant	___ Rash
40 ___ Compromising	___ Critical	___ Crafty	___ Changeable

PERSONALITY SCORING SHEET

Name

STRENGTHS

	SANGUINE	CHOLERIC	MELANCHOLY	PHLEGMATIC
1	Animated	Adventurous	Analytical	Adaptable
2	Playful	Persuasive	Persistent	Peaceful
3	Sociable	Strong-willed	Self-sacrificing	Submissive
4	Convincing	Competitive	Considerate	Controlled
5	Refreshing	Resourceful	Respectful	Reserved
6	Spirited	Self-reliant	Sensitive	Satisfied
7	Promoter	Positive	Planner	Patient
8	Spontaneous	Sure	Scheduled	Shy
9	Optimistic	Outspoken	Orderly	Obliging
10	Funny	Forceful	Faithful	Friendly
11	Delightful	Daring	Detailed	Diplomatic
12	Cheerful	Confident	Cultured	Consistent
13	Inspiring	Independent	Idealistic	Inoffensive
14	Demonstrative	Decisive	Deep	Dry humor
15	Mixes easily	Mover	Musical	Mediator
16	Talker	Tenacious	Thoughtful	Tolerant
17	Lively	Leader	Loyal	Listener
18	Cute	Chief	Chartmaker	Contented
19	Popular	Productive	Perfectionist	Permissive
20	Bouncy	Bold	Behaved	Balanced

TOTALS _____ _____ _____ _____

WEAKNESSES

	SANGUINE	CHOLERIC	MELANCHOLY	PHLEGMATIC
21	Brassy	Bossy	Bashful	Blank
22	Undisciplined	Unsympathetic	Unforgiving	Unenthusiastic
23	Repetitious	Resistant	Resentful	Reluctant
24	Forgetful	Frank	Fussy	Fearful
25	Interrupts	Impatient	Insecure	Indecisive
26	Unpredictable	Unaffectionate	Unpopular	Uninvolved
27	Haphazard	Headstrong	Hard-to-please	Hesitant
28	Permissive	Proud	Pessimistic	Plain
29	Angered easily	Argumentative	Alienated	Aimless
30	Naïve	Nervy	Negative attitude	Nonchalant
31	Wants credit	Workaholic	Withdrawn	Worrier
32	Talkative	Tactless	Too sensitive	Timid
33	Disorganized	Domineering	Depressed	Doubtful
34	Inconsistent	Intolerant	Introvert	Indifferent
35	Messy	Manipulative	Moody	Mumbles
36	Show-off	Stubborn	Skeptical	Slow
37	Loud	Lord-over-others	Loner	Lazy
38	Scatter-brained	Short tempered	Suspicious	Sluggish
39	Restless	Rash	Revengeful	Reluctant
40	Changeable	Crafty	Critical	Compromising

TOTALS _____ _____ _____ _____

COMBINED
TOTALS _____ _____ _____ _____

STRENGTHS

	The Talker **SANGUINE**	*The Worker* **CHOLERIC**
E M O T I O N S	Appealing personality Talkative, story teller Life of the party Good sense of humor Memory for color Physically holds onto listener Emotional and demonstrative Enthusiastic and expressive Cheerful and bubbling over Curious Good on stage Wide-eyed and innocent Lives in the present Changeable disposition Sincere at heart Always a child	Born leader Dynamic and active Compulsive need for change Must correct wrongs Strong-willed and decisive Unemotional Not easily discouraged Independent and self-sufficient Exudes confidence Can run anything
W O R K	Volunteers for jobs Thinks up new activities Looks great on the surface Creative and colorful Has energy and enthusiasm Starts in a flashy way Inspires others to join Charms others to work	Goal-oriented Sees the whole picture Organizes well Seeks practical solutions Moves quickly to action Delegates work Insists on production Makes the goal Stimulates activity Thrives on opposition
F R I E N D S	Makes friends easily Loves people Thrives on compliments Seems exciting Envied by others Doesn't hold grudges Apologizes quickly Prevents dull moments Likes spontaneous activities	Has little need for friends Will work for group activity Will lead and organize Is usually right Excels in emergencies

STRENGTHS

	The Thinker **MELANCHOLY**	*The Watcher* **PHLEGMATIC**
E M O T I O N S	Deep and thoughtful Analytical Serious and purposeful Talented and creative Artistic or musical Philosophical and poetic Appreciative of beauty Sensitive to others Self-sacrificing Conscientious Idealistic	Low-key personality Easygoing and relaxed Calm, cool, and collected Patient, well-balanced Consistent life Quiet, but witty Sympathetic and kind Keeps emotions hidden Happily reconciled to life All-purpose person
W O R K	Schedule-oriented Perfectionist, high standards Detail conscious Persistent and thorough Orderly and organized Neat and tidy Economical Sees the problems Finds creative solutions Needs to finish what he starts Likes charts, graphs, figures, lists	Competent and steady Peaceful and agreeable Has administrative ability Mediates problems Avoids conflicts Good under pressure Finds the easy way
F R I E N D S	Makes friends cautiously Content to stay in background Avoids causing attention Faithful and devoted Will listen to complaints Can solve others' problems Deep concern for other people Moved to tears with compassion Seeks ideal mate	Easy to get along with Pleasant and enjoyable Inoffensive Good listener Dry sense of humor Enjoys watching people Has many friends Has compassion and concern

WEAKNESSES

	The Talker **SANGUINE**	The Worker **CHOLERIC**
E M O T I O N S	Compulsive talker Exaggerates and elaborates Dwells on trivia Can't remember names Scares others off Too happy for some Has restless energy Egotistical Blusters and complains Naïve, gets taken in Has loud voice and laugh Controlled by circumstances Gets angry easily Seems phony to some Never grows up	Bossy Impatient Quick-tempered Can't relax Too impetuous Enjoys controversy & arguments Won't give up when losing Comes on too strong Inflexible Is not complimentary Dislikes tears and emotions Is unsympathetic
W O R K	Would rather talk Forgets obligations Doesn't follow through Confidence fades fast Undisciplined Priorities out of order Decides by feelings Easily distracted Wastes time talking	Little tolerance for mistakes Doesn't analyze details Bored by trivia May make rash decisions May be rude or tactless Manipulates people Demanding of others End justifies the means Work may become his god Demands loyalty in the ranks
F R I E N D S	Hates to be alone Needs to be center stage Wants to be popular Looks for credit Dominates conversation Interrupts and doesn't listen Answers for others Fickle and forgetful Makes excuses Repeats stories	Tends to use people Dominates others Decides for others Knows everything Can do everything better Is too independent Possessive of friends and mate Can't say "I'm sorry" May be right, but unpopular

WEAKNESSES

	The Thinker **MELANCHOLY**	*The Watcher* **PHLEGMATIC**
E M O T I O N S	Remembers the negatives Moody and depressed Enjoys being hurt Has false humility Off in another world Low self-image Has selective hearing Self-centered Too introspective Guilt feelings Persecution complex Tends to hypochondria	Unenthusiastic Fearful and worried Indecisive Avoids responsibility Quiet will of iron Selfish Too shy and reticent Too compromising Self-righteous
W O R K	Not people-oriented Depressed over imperfections Chooses difficult work Hesitant to start projects Spends too much time planning Prefers analysis to work Self-deprecating Hard to please Standards often too high Deep need for approval	Not goal-oriented Lacks self-motivation Hard to get moving Resents being pushed Lazy and careless Discourages others Would rather watch
F R I E N D S	Lives through others Insecure socially Withdrawn and remote Critical of others Holds back affection Dislikes those in opposition Suspicious of people Antagonistic and vengeful Unforgiving Full of contradictions Skeptical of compliments	Dampens enthusiasm Stays uninvolved Is not exciting Indifferent to plans Judges others Sarcastic and teasing Resists change

Notes

1. James 1:24 TLB.
2. Shakespeare, *As You Like It*, Act III, sc. 7.
3. Philippians 2:2-4 TEV.
4. Edgar Snow, *Journey to the Beginning*.
5. William Shakespeare, *Measure for Measure,* Act II, sc. 2.
6. William Shakespeare, *Twelfth Night,* Act II, sc. 5.
7. *San Bernardino Sun*, April 15, 1984.
8. Shakespeare, *Measure for Measure*, Act III, sc. 1.
9. Romans 5:2-4.
10. 2 Corinthians 5.
11. Church of the Woods, Lake Arrowhead, CA.
12. See John 8:7.
13. James 1:8,6.
14. See Romans 7:19.
15. Matthew 19:26.
16. "This Thing Is from Me" (Grand Rapids, MI: Faith, Prayer and Tract League).
17. *Time*, April 9, 1984, p.78.
18. Robert Burns, "To a Louse," stanza 8.
19. Proverbs 16:18.
20. 1 Corinthians 10:12.
21. Psalm 66:1,2,4.
22. John 15:16.
23. Acts 10:36.
24. Jeremiah 3:15.
25. Proverbs 10:20 TLB.
26. Ezekiel 34:2 TLB.
27. 1 Corinthians 14:40.
28. Matthew 7:1,2.
29. Ephesians 4:29.
30. Matthew 5:28.
31. Proverbs 10:10 TLB.
32. Isaiah 5:21.

33. Romans 12:10,13,3; 13:5 TEV.
34. Psalm 49:6.
35. Philippians 4:6,7.
36. Isaiah 26:3.
37. Hebrews 10:36 TEV.
38. Luke 10:41 TEV.
39. Matthew 6:3,4 TEV.
40. Proverbs 10:26 TLB.
41. Proverbs 12:24 TLB.
42. Haggai 2:4.
43. 2 Timothy 2:24.
44. 1 Corinthians 13:11.
45. Ephesians 4:16 TEV.
46. See Ephesians 5:28.
47. 2 Corinthians 4:16 TEV.
48. Proverbs 18:24.
49. 1 Corinthians 13:4,5 TLB.
50. Proverbs 11:13 TLB.
51. Proverbs 16:28 TLB.
52. 1 Timothy 3:11 TEV.
53. Proverbs 10:19 TLB.
54. Proverbs 16:24 TLB.
55. Proverbs 11:22 TLB.
56. Jeremiah 31:34.
57. Matthew 6:14.
58. Mark 11:25.
59. Luke 17:4.
60. Ephesians 4:32.
61. Philippians 2:13 TEV.
62. Philemon 1-3 TEV.
63. Philemon 4 TEV.
64. Philippians 4:8.
65. See Philippians 2:5-8.
66. Matthew 5:9.

Other Books by Florence Littauer

Personality Plus
Put Power in Your Personality!
Taking Charge of Your Life
It Takes So Little to Be Above Average
I've Found My Keys, Now Where's My Car?
Silver Boxes
Dare to Dream
Raising Christians, Not Just Children
Your Personality Tree (also available as video album)
Hope for Hurting Women
Looking for God in All the Right Places
The Gift of Encouraging Words

After Every Wedding Comes a Marriage with Fred Littauer
Freeing Your Mind from Memories that Bind with Fred Littauer
Daily Marriage Builders with Fred Littauer
Why Do I Feel the Way I Do? with Fred Littauer

Getting Along with Almost Anybody with Marita Littauer
Personality Puzzle with Marita Littauer
Talking So People Will Listen with Marita Littauer

CLASS Books

Christian Leaders, Authors, and Speakers Seminars (tape, album, and manual)
The Best of Florence Littauer